THINGS
YOU CAN DO
WHEN YOU'RE DEAD!

THINGS
YOU CAN DO
WHEN YOU'RE DEAD!

TRUE ACCOUNTS OF AFTER
DEATH COMMUNICATION

by

TRICIA J. ROBERTSON

www.whitecrowbooks.com

Things You Can Do When You're Dead!

Published and printed in the United States of America and the United Kingdom by White Crow Books; an imprint of White Crow Productions Ltd.

For information, contact White Crow Books
at 3 Merrow Grange, Guildford GU1 2QW United Kingdom,
or e-mail to info@whitecrowbooks.com.

Cover Designed by Butterflyeffect
Interior production by essentialworks.co.uk
Interior design by Perseus-Design.com

Paperback ISBN 978-1-908733-60-3
eBook   ISBN 978-1-908733-61-0

Non Fiction / Body, Mind & Spirit / Death & Dying

www.whitecrowbooks.com

In this book, one of Scotland's most experienced psychic investigators draws upon her extensive knowledge of cases involving apparitions, poltergeists, mediumship, reincarnation and paranormal healing to present the evidence for survival. What makes this a particularly valuable work is the large number of cases presented, many of which have been investigated by the author personally and never been published before. The informal, chatty style makes the accounts both gripping and easy to read.

—PROFESSOR BERNARD CARR, PAST PRESIDENT OF THE SOCIETY FOR PSYCHICAL RESEARCH AND CHAIR OF THE SCIENTIFIC AND MEDICAL NETWORK

Tricia Robertson is one of those rare field researchers who have a way of discovering new cases, investigating them thoroughly, and writing them up in a highly readable way. There is some remarkable material here, and it makes for absorbing reading.

—GUY LYON PLAYFAIR, AUTHOR OF THIS HOUSE IS HAUNTED AND TWIN TELEPATHY

Tricia J Robertson draws on many of her own experiences as a psychical researcher in this excellent, easily read, book which is ideal for anyone who is seeking genuine examples of after death communication and almost reads like a thriller, in the sense of 'What is going to happen next?'

—DR DAVID HAMILTON, AUTHOR OF IT'S THE THOUGHT THAT COUNTS AND IS YOUR LIFE MAPPED OUT?

An engaging and informative introduction to the topic of post mortem survival.

—PROFESSOR STEPHEN BRAUDE, AUTHOR OF IMMORTAL REMAINS AND FIRST PERSON PLURAL

CONTENTS

This book is dedicated to my children, Martin and Roslyn, for putting up with a 'strange' mother for all of these years.

ACKNOWLEDGEMENTS

I acknowledge the debt of gratitude that we all owe to the historical work done in psychical research, by many intellectual giants.

On a personal level I have been fortunate to know many of them and would like to acknowledge their support throughout the years.

In 1994 a research organisation was set up named P.R.I.S.M. (Psychical Research Involving Selected Mediums). This was set up to combine the talents of psychical researchers and mediums in order that we could design experiments to try to further the understanding of the processes involved in the transfer of mediumship information. The mediums were as enthusiastic about this as the researchers. Everyone worked for no financial recompense.

Many of the original members of council have now passed over, the latest, at this time, being my dearest colleague Professor Archie Roy, who passed in December 2012.

Archie was a tower of enthusiasm and strength to me and I will always treasure and appreciate that fact.

There are so many eminent people to acknowledge, but I also wish to particularly recognise the contributions made to psychical research by Professor David Fontana, Montague Keen, Maurice Grosse and Professor Arthur Ellison, four of the original PRISM members and Guy Lyon Playfair who joined us at a later date.

INTRODUCTION

Although the title of this book appears to be flippant, the contents are certainly not. It addresses serious questions such as 'Who are we as human beings?' 'What talents, latent or otherwise, might we have?' and 'Is there life after death?' The evidence contained in this book would appear to point to the fact that 'you can't die for the life of you'.

This book is aimed, not at experienced psychical researchers, but at the ordinary person in the street who may not have read any in-depth literature on the subject of human survival after death.

I will illustrate and discuss subjects such as apparitions, poltergeist phenomena, drop-in communicators, aspects of mediumship information, reincarnation, paranormal healing, and psychic surgery and consider who, and maybe what, we are as human beings.

Do we have latent abilities that lie untapped? Does everyone have access to these abilities?

The contents of this book should not detract from anyone's religious beliefs, but possibly add to them. Similarly anyone of an agnostic persuasion is free to interpret the events and phenomena in any way that they wish.

Is there a part of us that is separate from our physical bodies and brain? Is that the part of us that continues after death? Does that part still display individual personal knowledge, memories, emotion, personality traits and intelligence for logical thought?

After reading this book, you will be in a better position to make your own judgement. Everything written here is done with 100% honesty. If you had told me 30 years ago that I would be writing such a book, I would have thought that you were mad. But as a former science teacher I have had to go where the evidence leads and much of the evidence would imply that there is more to life than our physical existence. Of course there are claims of paranormality which are false or ill perceived, but that does not negate the genuine cases. It is good to remember that there are counterfeit coins going around, but that does not mean that all coins are counterfeit.

Chapter 1

DEATH

Just because you no longer have a physical body does not mean that you cannot function. If you thought that your hard work was over when you died then I'm afraid that evidence would point to the idea that this may not indeed be true. As someone who has investigated these matters for over thirty years I can share my experiences and findings with you. This book contains events that actually happened. If you think that I am deluded then think again and, for a start, consider the following quotations from two great thinkers.

> Human history is based on assuming a rather humdrum world in which we know all the rules. Change one aspect, and – presto! We are perched on a precarious world view.
>
> PROFESSOR GREGORY BENFORD

> Those who assume that we are now acquainted with all, or nearly all, or even with any assignable proportion, of the forces that work in the universe, show a limitation of conception which ought to be impossible in an age when the widening of the circle of our definite knowledge does but reveal the proportionally widening circle of our blank, absolute indubitable ignorance.
>
> PROFESSOR SIR WILLIAM CROOKES

From experience, I estimate that about one in five people have had an 'anomalous' experience, or know of a close friend who has. I am not suggesting for a second that all such experiences come from those departed, but some would indicate that the most parsimonious explanation for the experience is that it has been produced or instigated by someone deceased. The study of such matters is called Psychical Research. In 1882 a society was set up in London by eminent thinkers of the time and their objective was to study these things in as scientific a manner as possible. This society is called The Society for Psychical Research. By the very nature of these 'anomalous' experiences, they are pragmatic and experiential and as such can only be judged as in a court of law that is 'beyond reasonable doubt': the most difficult word in the last sentence being 'reasonable'. Something may seem reasonable to one person and not another, as in the jury system.

History has shown that the scientific establishment has always spurned or neglected the unconventional, the innovator and the 'new thinker' only to eventually accept, perhaps grudgingly, his or her discoveries in the end. In this respect the wise words of Marx - not Karl but Groucho – may be relevant.

> 'They said Galileo was mad when he claimed the Earth revolved round the Sun - but it does. They said Wilbur and Orville Wright were out of their minds when they said men could fly - but they did. They said my uncle Waldorf was crazy - and he was as mad as a hatter!'

In other words we have to examine every reported account of anomalous phenomena in its own right, judging each and every case on its own merit. (Or demerit)

This can cause huge problems to the public in general, as avid critics, determined in their own mind that these things just cannot happen, usually holds up and publicises a weak case and says something like 'You see there is no substance to these claims', neglecting others which are hard to ignore, accept and understand.

As a point of interest, towards the end of the Victorian era, the first glimpses of the micro world of atomic physics, beneath the hard billiard ball atoms of the nineteenth century, was revealed by scientists like Lord Rutherford, Sir Joseph J.Thomson, Lord Rayleigh and others also operating for the most part out of sheer curiosity and little caring whether or not their discoveries would ever be applicable. "One thing of which you can be absolutely certain", Rutherford commented about his early experiments in atom-smashing, "this will have no practical use whatsoever." I pass no comment.

So who knows where our studies of 'afterlife' may lead us?

As already stated, we will look at the question "What are we, as human beings, what latent talents might we possess and, more importantly, is there any evidence that our personality persists, along with all of our human knowledge, memories and experience, when we die?" If we do survive, what kind of evidence would satisfy us, here on Earth, that this is the case?

If a friend of yours telephones you from a strange landline - how do you know that it is that person speaking? I ask you to think about that, it may be someone playing a joke on you and pretending to be that person or it may indeed be that person. How would you judge? In this there seems to be a parallel with some post mortem communications. So what would satisfy you?

Receiving information that only you and the deceased person would know?

Receiving information from an alleged deceased person that you did not know and have to check?

Seeing an apparition?

Speaking to an apparition?

Witnessing poltergeist type of activity?

Hearing the voice of a deceased person?

Hearing a person give an evidential account of an identifiable former life?

Seeing a person, with no medical background, diagnose and give successful healing to a person?

Everyone will have their own opinion about what is acceptable to them.

Let us start with Apparitions.

Chapter 2

APPARITIONS

I am not going to talk about the historical type of apparition as in an old castle or battle site, but modern experiences by people who are of sound mind and body. The critic will correctly say that some people see an apparition due to the taking of alcohol, drugs, medication, trauma etc. and that these experiences are not 'real'. This may be true, but the cases cited here do not involve any of the aforementioned parameters.

Since the early days of the SPR accounts of apparitions have been recorded from all over the world and in no small number. Many surveys of apparitional experiences have been carried out, even in recent years, and in days gone by the SPR itself set out a study called 'The Census of Hallucinations' which included thousands of people as participants and employed over 400 people to collect the data. This was a huge undertaking. Professor Erlendur Haraldsson from Iceland has also carefully studied this phenomenon for many years, and has published a paper citing 450 such cases in Iceland. He has many cases documented where the apparition has appeared to a person he never met while alive. This is probably due to the fact that fishing is a common occupation in Iceland and most of the Icelandic apparitions are of young fishermen who drowned. In these cases the percipients (the people who saw the apparitions) subsequently had to make inquiry from the information given by the apparition to validate the identity.

There have been many actual studies of apparitions, one of these by G.N.M.Tyrrell from the SPR in which he classified apparitions into four categories: experimental, post mortem, crisis and haunt.

Experimental: There have been occasions where living people have deliberately tried to make themselves known to another by projecting themselves in some way as an apparition. Apparently this can be done.

Post Mortem: As the title suggests an apparition is seen after the death of a person. It could be 5 minutes after death or fifty years.

Crisis: Whereby an apparition of a person is seen at the point of death or undergoing a great crisis. This seemingly happens a lot during times of war, where the 'apparition' is far away from family.

Haunt: When an apparition is seen under any other circumstance.

An apparition may appear to someone in semi-solid form and the percipient can "see through" it, or at least the part that has been materialised. Although the basic shape and some features are defined and recognisable, sometimes these figures do not materialise fully. On other occasions an apparition can appear as a solid, fully formed, living person, so much so that the percipient accepts it as a living being. The following represents such an account.

Captain Bob

In the month of June 1995, an airline captain flew as an ordinary passenger from Heathrow Airport London to Glasgow Airport on a pleasant sunny afternoon; the plane touched down at 2.30pm. He had been in Budapest during the previous week on potential business, flying Eastern European aeroplanes, before spending a few days in Cambridge.

In any given account of paranormal events it is always wise to check or observe the credibility of the witness or witnesses. A trained observer or any type of expert witness does add weight to any given account.

To let you understand the quality of this eyewitness to a paranormal phenomenon, his background is as follows.

Captain Robert B. Hambleton – Jones, married and with one child, was born in Warrington but moved to Derbyshire at the age of one. He is one of a family of six children. His senior school education was completed at Lady Manners School, Bakewell. According to his mother he was obsessed with the thought of piloting an aeroplane from the age of three. He sat and passed the Civil Service Commissioners' examination for entrance to the Britannia Royal Naval College, Dartmouth. After six months he was seconded to the R.A.F for flying training in order that he might qualify as a Fleet Air Arm pilot. After completing flying training and obtaining his "wings of gold" he proceeded to operational flying training at fighter squadron 738 at RNAS Lossiemouth, Scotland where he graduated from the night fighter training squadron with the highest first class assessment ever given, to that date. Subsequently he served as a pilot in several night fighter squadrons, based on an aircraft carrier, and was involved with day and night missions for five years. He then trained at RNAS as an air warfare instructor and served on HMS Ark Royal on the Beira Patrol during the U.D.I. incident in Rhodesia. In 1966 he was chosen to serve with the Top Gun squadron VF121 at Miramar, California for just over two years, prior to the delivery of the extraordinary Phantom F4 all weather fighter aircraft, which the Royal Navy purchased from the McDonnell Douglas Corporation in the USA. After two years at the Top Gun Squadron as an instructor on the F4 he returned to the United Kingdom to join the first British F4 squadron. Having served a total of twelve years in the Royal Navy, he then retired from this line of work. In fact the film "Top Gun" showed one office in the movie which was in reality Bob's office. We now rib him that he is not as good-looking as Tom Cruise.

As you can imagine, this type of flying required nerves of steel, a good logical mind and involved a high degree of observational skills. Captain Bob met all of these requirements. During his time of service he saw many people die, including some of his colleagues. This is not a man given to fabrication of the truth, ephemeral ideas or flights of fancy.

At Glasgow airport on the day in question he was half expecting to be picked up and driven home by a friend who said that he would try to be there. Upon Bob's arrival in the terminal building there was no sign of his friend and after waiting a good few minutes he then crossed the concourse within the building, put down his bag and checked his wristwatch; it was 2.45pm. He looked up in the vain hope that the friend would appear but as he visually searched his eye was caught by another man with a huge grin on his face coming diagonally towards him across the concourse. This man was looking directly at Bob's face as he walked across from one set of sliding doors at the airport entrance. It was not the friend that he had expected but he recognised him as another Captain, an ex-colleague from another airline where they had worked in the same time period for several years after Bob left the Navy. This man, let's call

7

him Jack, was approximately 20 years younger than him but they had always been great friends and Bob was delighted to see him. However he could not help but notice that the younger man had lost, as he put it, " a hellova lot of weight." It had been at least nine months since he had last seen him and he was quite taken aback by his very thin appearance, although of course he said nothing. As Jack greeted him with phrases like "How are you, you old b----r" - they chatted for a short time: the only thing that Bob thought slightly odd was that Jack never put his hand out to shake hands as he would normally have done, but he didn't think too much of it. After the exchange of pleasantries Jack said "Must go I'm late" and rushed towards the line at the end checkout, obviously travelling as a passenger on the flight boarding at that checkout at that time. Bob picked up his bag, had a good smile to himself, and took a couple of steps forward before looking back to catch another glimpse of his friend. He did not actually see him and thought that he must have really rushed through the checkout, but yet again did not think anything strange about this. The other friend who was supposed to pick him up did not make an appearance, and therefore Bob had to catch a bus home, no doubt muttering under his breath.

The next morning he went down to his local pub, one which was used regularly by lawyers and pilots, for a drink. He was minding his own business when someone said to him "You must know this man" and a "Scotsman" newspaper was plonked in front of him on the table. As he looked at it he saw a largish picture of the face of Jack, whom he had met on the previous day, and was trying to read the text when it suddenly hit him that above the photograph was the word "Obituary." He was furious. He thought that someone had made a terrible mistake, or worse, was playing a sick joke, and was so upset that he telephoned the airline company for whom Jack worked to ask them what they were playing at, only to discover that Jack had died very unexpectedly two days earlier in an Edinburgh hospital. He was only 38 years old.

For several days Bob wandered around stunned and in a dazed condition not knowing what to make of this at all, until eventually through a friend, Carol, he managed to contact myself and Professor Archie Roy. It was obvious that he was emotionally shattered by the experience, as at times he was reduced to tears while recounting the events. This man had no religious belief or predisposition for accepting the phenomenon of this type of event and he was totally bemused. In actual fact he hated the whole idea of a 'God' scenario. Our task was then to investigate his account.

As my colleague and co-investigator, Professor Archie Roy, had to go to Italy to direct a NATO Advanced Study Institute I took up the case and set up a visit with the head of security at Glasgow Airport, who turned out to be wonderfully helpful. It was established that the security videotape of that date, place and time had been wiped and reused.

The head of security then handed me a flight schedule, and upon checking aeroplane timetables for that day we discovered that there was a flight to Jack's small hometown at 3.00pm on the day in question and the checkout desk for that flight was the end desk which Bob saw his friend running towards. (It is worth noting again that Bob checked his watch at 2.45pm). The chief of security also established, subsequently, that the coffin of an airline pilot was transported through Glasgow Airport about that time and certainly on that day, having been already transferred from Edinburgh. Although we cannot pinpoint the exact time of this coffin transfer we know for certain that it was loaded on to an aircraft bound for Jack's hometown destination on that day. One possible answer to this mystery would have been if Jack had a twin brother or a brother who looked exactly like him, and who also knew Bob, but he did not. No other person with even the same surname was on board that 3 o'clock flight.

Upon subsequent investigation, it transpired that Jack had been quite ill for the previous 6 months and had lost three stones in weight during that time. He had been admitted to a hospital in Edinburgh for tests but things took a turn for the worse and he sadly died there. If you remember, the first thing that Bob noticed was that Jack had lost a lot of weight. As they had not met for a good nine months, due mostly to wide-spread work commitments for separate companies, there would be absolutely no way that Bob could have known about this. This evidence of weight loss somewhat shattered his own hope that he had made some sort of weird mistake, but this veridical information tying in with Jack's physical appearance made a mistake less plausible.

When Bob discovered this fact he was stunned and he looked physically shattered and bewildered when we were given this information. He had been a total agnostic and did not believe in any of this "rubbish"; I use rubbish as a euphemism. Nevertheless he was still searching for a logical answer regarding the encounter with his "friend".

Now if we examine the account:

> Jack walked diagonally across the concourse, from one set of sliding doors at the entrance, grinning all over his face, and made his way towards Bob.

Jack had a very unusual gap between his teeth, which made him highly distinguishable from other person. He also wore gold spectacles that were a very unusual size in that they were very large and almost looked too big for his face.

Having come from Edinburgh, a coffin was transported through Glasgow Airport roughly about the same time, certainly on the same day, as the two men met. Remember that Jack died in an Edinburgh hospital two days earlier.

The destination of the coffin was Jack's hometown. Although he had lost all that weight, he would have had no expectation of dying at that time.

Bob did not know that his friend had lost weight, or even that he had been poorly.

A good test of a case is the effect that the phenomenon has had on the recipient.

When I last spoke to Bob, some nine years later, he stated that he "knows who he bloody well met on that day." As this case has had quite a lot of media exposure, there has been ample time for someone to come forward and shed some light on this topic if, for example, there had been an error in his identification of Jack.

As Bob was an agnostic, to say the least, he has since had to rethink about his model of reality, a task that he still does not find easy or pleasurable. There is absolutely no doubt of his sincerity and his assertion holds to this day as to the identity of the phantom pilot.

I can hear the sceptic now saying "Oh he just made a mistake"
How does the sceptic know that he just made a mistake?

Although this would be the most parsimonious of explanations, how would the sceptic explain the three stone weight loss; a coffin containing an airline pilot's body going through the airport at approximately the same time as Bob's encounter; a pilot's coffin being loaded onto a flight which was headed for Jack's hometown destination; the fact that a plane was heading out to Jack's hometown destination, a very small place at that, at that particular time?

Another very important point is that the men recognised each other and had a correspondingly suitable conversation. It would be very strange indeed if this "mistaken" Jack had Jack's knowledge and was also identical to his ex-colleague in physical appearance.

Do you think it was a mistake?

If this was the only account of such a happening we may easily try to dismiss even this case, but there are thousands of well authenticated, similar occurrences. In fact, apart from a few jibes from some people that he has met since then, there have been many more people who have shared somewhat similar experiences with Bob, no doubt secure in the knowledge that he would not laugh at them.

The experience did not cheer Bob up any as it somewhat shattered his model of life and death. Strangely enough he said that he knew the experience to be real but he could still not accept the idea of survival. I believe that is called a catch 22 situation.

A Fright At a Height

The following account relates to another solid apparition, but with one difference.

A shopkeeper of reliable reputation, who was already known to me, was redecorating a room in his home while the rest of the family were away on holiday. He lives in an old style detached red sandstone property of the type that has extremely high ceilings. He had no real interest or any great knowledge of the paranormal at all until he had the following experience.

To use his words;

"I was painting, quite happily, stretching out at the highest point of a bedroom ceiling when suddenly my attention was caught by a man looking at me, just four feet away from my face. The level of his head was similar to my own, just inches under the ceiling." After the initial shock he then noted that the man appeared to be solid but was only visible from his waist level to the top of his head - a man whom he then recognised as being a customer who used to come into his shop from some time back and he instantly recalled the man's name. He saw clearly that the man was wearing an olive green shirt, a tie and a tweed jacket, and that his face was in full colour and totally lifelike. This man had a rosy complexion and nicely coloured cheeks. In life he had had the "life and soul of the party" type of personality and even now he looked no different. (The bit that he could see anyway!)

This man then pointed at him and spoke in a very animated manner and said, "Tell them not to do it, everything will be all right". As the shopkeeper was still in a state of disbelief and shock he has no idea of how long he stared at this person. The statement was repeated adamantly, while the man's finger still pointed and gesticulated at him, "Tell them not to do it, everything will be all right" and then the man disappeared instantly, just as quickly as he had appeared. He did not fade away gradually, just gone, all at once.

Shaking with the shock and disbelief of what had just happened, the shopkeeper came down the ladder very slowly as he was in grave danger of falling off it and he was unable to do any more work that evening. In fact it took him quite some time before he could stop shaking enough to make himself a cup of tea. He actually had some comments to make which, for decency's sake, cannot be printed in this book.

He thought back and realised that this man had died over six years ago and his widow continued to patronise his shop. He was stunned by the whole event. The next day he attended his shop as usual and was happy to forget the events of the previous evening; however the following day the widow of the "apparition" came into the shop and this posed a serious problem – should he tell her or not about his experience? He eventually decided that he should tell her and asked her to come into the back of the shop where, with much trepidation, he plucked up the courage to tell her of the events. It was most likely done in self-defence as he probably thought that if he did not pass on the information the "man" might come back again.

When he had finished telling the lady her reaction was totally unexpected, she threw her arms around him and thanked him while saying that she had already been given similar information by someone else, and this confirmed it. He was bewildered, as he did not have a clue as to what it was all about.

About two weeks later this lady asked him if she could speak with him in the back shop and she offered an explanation for the previous events. It transpired that her son had been wrongly accused of a crime, but the evidence was such that, if found guilty, he could have been given a jail sentence in an adult jail, as he was now, in law, considered to be an adult. The family did not want this to happen and had thought of taking him to Southern Ireland to hide, which would obviously mean that he would not appear at court and equally that he would not be able to return to Scotland again. Had they taken this action the young man would be in trouble with the authorities for the rest of his life.

However, the woman took the "advice" from her husband (via the shopkeeper) and when the boy did appear in court the following week (after the message) the case was admonished by the judge, very much against their own fears about the evidence which was to be presented. The judge simply said "No case to answer."

Remember the advice "Tell them not to do it – everything will be all right".

The shopkeeper has never experienced anything like this before or after this event. I know his character to be that of an honest and trustworthy person.

In case the sceptics think that he rushed to tell me of this account, he did not. It was only after a chance conversation with him that I had the ability to examine this case and these details emerged and he only gave them to me in the knowledge that we would not think that he had gone completely crazy.

As opposed to the Captain Bob case, where the apparition appeared to be absolutely natural, this one was not. The fact that the lower half of the body was missing and he appeared 4/6 inches under the ceiling was to say the least, unusual.

From a Distance

Each reported case of paranormal phenomena is quite different to any other, although there may be some seeming similarities. The possible causes of phenomena are like human beings themselves, individual in character and dependant on circumstances and other factors.

I once investigated a reported case of phenomenal events that spanned a distance of roughly 300 miles.

The household that I attended was a really beautiful detached house, which was wonderfully furnished, and it also had a superb ambience. The family consisted of husband, wife and two children; all of them were lovely people. If anything at all was unusual, it appeared as though the husband wanted to keep out of my way. (Maybe not that unusual then!)

The lady of the house, Jean, had a sister who lived in the South of England. This sister, Angela, had two children, a girl of 16 and a boy of 12. About three weeks prior to our visit, Jean's sister had died by her own hand having taken her life in her own home.

Because they had not been living in England for any length of time, Angela's daughter had really only made one good friend, Donna, whom she had met at school. A day or so after the tragedy of Angela's death, Donna's mother awakened during the night to see a figure of a woman standing at the foot of her bed. The woman was crying, she held her hands out and looked as though she was trying to speak, but did not speak. Donna's mother was fascinated and not upset or afraid by this and just continued to observe the appearance of the woman. She was about 5 feet 5 inches tall and had shoulder length blonde hair. Eventually the apparition disappeared and the lady cannot estimate, even now, the length of time that she was visible.

In the morning she asked Donna to describe the lady who had taken her own life, as she had never met her, although she had heard of Angela from her daughter. After hearing her daughter's description she was almost certain that this was the lady who had appeared to her the previous evening. As she and Donna were mesmerized and puzzled by this happening they did not mention it to anyone else. About a week or so later, "Angela" appeared again to Donna's mother. This time she was not crying and she spoke to say that she was concerned about her daughter's present behaviour. She explained that she did not like some of the things that her daughter was now doing, which included imbibing in alcoholic drink and taking soft drugs.

She asked the lady to tell the girl of her visit and to impress upon her that she was anxious to persuade her not to continue in this manner. The lady and her daughter did not know, at this point, that Donna's friend had a problem of this nature, but upon subsequent investigation the information proved to be correct. They invited the girl to their home and told her the whole story, and I understand that this did the trick as far as her behaviour was concerned.

Jean was amazed and confused by all of this and turned to me for advice and, if possible, help in trying to understand all that had transpired.

I was given permission and the information to contact the lady who had seen the apparitions of Angela. I spoke to the lady twice and she seemed a very ordinary, genuine person with no thought of glory, fame, fortune or anything of the sort. She was wondering why she should be the one that Angela should come to, but it seemed fairly obvious to me that the link would have been made via the daughter's friendship with Donna.

If any of you have lost anyone under such tragic circumstances you will understand that we have found that the frequent reaction of friends and family in this type of situation is of the order of,

"Could we have done anything to stop this?"
"Was there some sign that we missed?"
"Why did I not see this coming?"

People torture themselves over this, and the answer is "No, there is nothing you could have done." If people have a mind to do this, then they will; it appears as if a kind of temporary madness seizes them and the self-destruct button is pushed.

As someone who investigates mediums and mediumship on a regular basis, I cannot tell you of the number of times I have heard a communication given to a recipient from someone who has taken their own life, which says" I am sorry for the grief I have caused, but I did not know what I was doing. The balance of my mind seemed to go." I have heard this in every corner of the UK from many different mediums.

After speaking with Jean and family for a good length of time she seemed a bit more settled about the whole affair, although still naturally sad about her sister. Once she understood that her sister was still, in some sense, alive and making herself known, it did seem to ease her tension about the whole affair. It would seem to me that, deep down, people have a latent fear that those who commit suicide are in some way condemned to "the bad fire" as it were and lost forever. Pragmatically, this does not seem to be the case as I have heard, as indicated previously, many communications from just such people who appear in some sense to be alive and well.

A few years ago I was giving a short talk before a medium was due to give a demonstration at a public meeting. Because of this I remained on the platform and could therefore see the tops of the heads of the audience while the medium demonstrated. During the demonstration the medium came to a woman who was unknown to either of us. The medium's first words were "I have your son here; he took his own life by hanging." The woman nodded. The medium continued with a lot of information which appeared to come from her son and which was, strangely, actually quite jovial for the most part. After the complete demonstration I happened to meet this woman and I said to her "Are you the lady who got the message from your son?" Her reply was "Yes, and it will be the first time in two years that I will have a good night's sleep!" I asked her why and she said that her church had told her that her son would burn in hellfire and damnation for eternity as he had taken his own life."

In Bishop Pike's book *On the Other Side*, he relates his experiences with the medium Ena Twigg, after the suicide of his son. I quote part of the son's communication;

"I failed the test - I am confused" followed by "God, I didn't know what I was doing, but when I got here I found that I wasn't such a failure as I thought. My nervous system failed." followed by "I wanted out. I've found there is no way out I wish I'd stayed to work out my problems in more familiar surroundings."

But all in all he showed by his manner of speaking that he was not distressed, only sorry, and according to him he would be allowed to make progress in his new location.

So we have looked at three 'different' apparitions in the sense that one was known to the percipient, appeared in an airport and seemed quite natural.

One was loosely known to the percipient, partially appeared in his own home, and the part that was seen also appeared natural.

The third apparition was unknown to the percipient and was not really 'solid.'

It would appear that the three personalities may have had different agendas, the last two wishing to convey a message to a living relative, whereas Jack was possibly, just possibly, following his body home. Could it be that he did not know that he was dead? Whatever the reason, he did not seem to wish to convey anything in particular to any other person.

Other types of Apparitions

Living fire

A young couple, who lived in an old styled house, decided to open up the fireplace in the lounge; it had been covered over since they had bought the premises. They thought that they would like to make a feature of it and have a "real" log fire. They put a lot of work into this and sat with pride as the first open fire was lit. Present in the room were the couple and the sister of the gentleman.

As the fire blazed gloriously the sister looked at her brother's face and said "You can see that, can't you?" He nodded in agreement as he stared at the fireplace. They both saw a young girl of about 10 years of age, kneeling in front of the fire with the palms of her hands held upwards, as if warming them at the fire. She wore a white dress and had a large blue bow tied in the back of her hair. Both witnesses saw exactly the same thing but the third person in the room saw nothing.

This child has never been seen again.

Most people who have a spontaneous paranormal experience really don't want to talk about it for fear of being thought a bit strange. That is why I find it interesting, and not surprising, that the man would almost certainly not even have mentioned that he could see the girl if his sister had not observed the expression on his face, one, which, at that exact time, corroborated her own experience of seeing the child. Just for the record, neither person had ever seen anything like this before this event, or has experienced anything resembling it since.

Roadway Apparition

An acquaintance of mine was having plasterwork carried out on the internal walls of his home. The gentleman overseeing this work was middle aged and just a typical no nonsense Glasgow worker, been there, done it and got the T-shirt. Before the strange event that occurred, he had indicated in an earlier conversation that he didn't believe a word of any spooky paranormal nonsense. He knew that my friend did and I think that he was announcing this and showing his macho outlook on life in case he became tainted in some way. One day, near the end of the plasterwork job, this man came in looking as white as a sheet. My friend inquired into the cause of his appearance.

The man reluctantly told him of an event that had taken place on the previous evening around twilight. As this occurred during the lighter nights, twilight was about 10.30pm. The man had hired a taxi to take him home about 10.00pm that night and was winging his way home in the back seat of the taxi as the driver drove him along a narrow, country type of, road towards his house. Suddenly the taxi driver yelled "Look at that idiot" at the driver of a car that was coming towards them on the wrong side of the road, heading straight towards the taxi. A collision seemed imminent. There was not enough room for two cars to pass each other and the taxi driver pulled over to the left of the road as far as he could and stopped. Both he and the passenger could only stare at the oncoming vehicle in horror. As they stared at the car nearly upon them it faded and disappeared right in front of their eyes, one second it was there and the next it had gone. They stuttered to each other with phrases such as "did you see that?" The taxi driver freaked out and it took some time for his nerves to settle before he was able to continue driving the rest of the journey to the passenger's house.

Sufficient to say that it gave both men something to think about.

Footsteps in The Snow

A trusted female acquaintance of mine related the following account to me.

Her husband, having worked late one evening, was taking his usual shortcut through a park on his way home. I will call him John. It was about 9.00pm. It so happened that during that day the first heavy snow of winter had fallen, in fact quite a few inches in a short time. The streets were deserted, as was the park, and the man noted how pretty and Christmas postcard-like everything looked as the streetlights were twinkling on the snow and a nearby pond looked idyllic. All at once he was aware of a man walking beside him and engaging him in conversation. He couldn't understand where the man had appeared from, but didn't give it much thought. The man chatted on and on and was actually getting on John's nerves, but he said nothing much in response, just monosyllabic utterances. The second man asked continuous questions such as inquiring into the number of children he had what they were getting for Christmas, and so on.

At this point the journey across the park had ended and as John turned to walk along a particular road he made to say goodbye to the second gent. Responding, the second man said that he was not in a hurry and would walk part of the way with him. Knowing that he would soon be home with his wife and children he thought that he could just about stand this man for that length of time, and made the best of it.

They were walking past a row of about 8 shops on the final leg of John's journey when, half way along this row of shops, the second man took his leave and both men said goodbye to each other.

John took a step forward, still uneasy in his mind as he was thinking that this other man had been a strange character and he was relieved to be rid of him, when almost automatically he turned around to see which way the man had gone. There was no one there. Amazed, he thought "but there is nowhere that he could have gone in that second or so" and was trying to puzzle it out when he looked down and then he noticed that there was only one set of footprints in the four inches of snow up to where he was standing. Not another print was to be seen as far as the eye could see. When his wife opened the door to him he was a nervous wreck, shaking and stuttering out the account beyond the hearing of the children. His wife wanted to put her coat on and go out with him to view the area, but he was so shaken that he would not go out again.

Now some of you may be thinking that this is just a story, but that man will not talk about the events now, and his wife knows the state that he was in when he arrived home. Yet again this man had no interest or belief in the paranormal. Incidentally, the man is a teetotaller, in case you are wondering if he was alcohol assisted.

These happenings do not appear to make much sense at all, but there will be an explanation for them, it is simply that we do not know what it is.

Dunbartonshire

By far, the most reported phenomenon to psychical researchers is that of a residency not being "quite" empty when a new owner or owners take over the property. Sometime after moving into such a new home they become aware of perhaps a "peculiar" feeling in the house which they cannot define, or items, on a regular basis, are not where they remembered leaving them. The next stage is usually that items sometimes disappear and appear in a different place or disappear and never re-appear. Now discounting the cases which may be nothing but imagination, there appear to be quite a few properties where the last resident has "gone on" bodily, but something has remained behind, call it what you will, their personality, energy, mind power or spirit. This "remainder" appears to interact in some measure with the incoming resident or residents. The following is such an account.

The householder concerned in this case asked me if I would visit to discuss reported happenings within the home. I knew no more than this when I arrived but was told by the lady in this household that her small child had been talking to a "lady", who could not be seen by herself or her husband. The child, who was a pretty little girl, spoke of the lady in her bedroom who kept her awake at night by speaking to her, and often the child would come out of bed through to the lounge crying, saying that she did not like this lady. There was a younger sister, but she was just a baby and was not affected by any disturbance. These events were happening nearly every night of the week and the child was becoming quite distraught. The father in particular did not like this at all. Even less did he like the thought of his wife calling people in to try to alleviate the problem. Someone had given the mother my contact number and after an initial conversation I made arrangements to visit and bring a medium, Mr Charles Morton, with me.

Upon our arrival it was obvious that the father eyed us with deep suspicion, always avoiding direct eye contact with us and walking nervously around as if trying to avoid any interaction with both of us. The little girl was a very bright three and a half year old, with no obvious inhibitions, who chatted away quite happily to us about ordinary matters as she assumed that we were just visitors. Much to the father's relief, I asked him if he could take the children away while we spoke to the mother about the situation, as I would not normally question small children about paranormal matters.

As the other child in the home was only a baby, you are now probably thinking, as I initially did, that perhaps the girl was looking for attention. Mother then elaborated on the previously reported events. The family had not long moved into the premises, which was a rather lovely bungalow. They were therefore new to the area but being a very nice family they had quickly made friends with a few neighbours.

It never fails to amaze me that people have the greatest common sense or call it intuition under the pressure which must be felt when paranormal phenomena occur. The mother had managed to tactfully extract information from a neighbour about the previous owner of the property. They themselves had never known the previous owner, as the house had been empty prior to their purchase of the property. It transpired that an elderly lady was the previous owner and she was said to be quite an acquisitive person.

Without being too obvious the mother of the child asked questions about this previous owner and expressed an interest in her appearance. Fortunately their neighbour, immediately next door, had a photograph of the lady that was taken a few years previously at a communal street function. The photograph contained about twenty-five people.

When the child first began to report that a lady was coming into her room at night her mother had asked the little girl to describe the lady. She said that she was a big lady with wee boobies. (Small breasts) By looking at the picture taken by the neighbour it was quite apparent that the previous owner matched the description, in this respect, that had been given by the child. Naturally the mother did not tell the neighbour why she was interested in a photograph of the previous owner and made no comment for fear of being thought loopy.

She asked to borrow the photo to show her husband, but in fact laid it on a table and later asked the child if she recognised anyone in the photograph. She immediately pointed and said 'That is the lady who comes into my room.'

Mr Morton was not told anything of the reported phenomena and was simply asked to 'tune in 'and see what he could pick up. He ostensibly contacted the previous owner and reported a similar description to the child. After some time he announced that she had been persuaded to move on and leave the house as she now realised that she had no need of it and that she had also been made aware that it was not correct that she should still be there.

Now I ask you to remember that the child knew nothing of this, she had gone with her father to the park and just thought that we were friends of her mother at home having a chat. After that day no further reports were made by the child that a lady was in her room. As I have said on many an occasion "the proof of the pudding is in the eating"

One incident that I must share with you is the fact that before we arrived the father had strong reservations about our visit, as he obviously did not know who or what to expect. He had nervously asked his wife if things would fly about the room when we arrived; I felt like Mary Poppins and found that statement amusing at first but was then saddened by the popular misconceptions of the paranormal and the investigations thereof.

About two weeks later I made contact with this family and was informed that all had been peaceful and quiet since our visit, and I have heard nothing since.

If this was the only account of such an event then you might feel that you have grounds to dismiss it, but there must be thousands upon thousands of similar accounts throughout the United Kingdom alone, each reported to different psychical researchers, ministers, priests and other organisations. The Church of England in fact has a healing diocese to deal with just such occasions and events.

It is very important to remember that each resident reporting an account, usually does not know of the accounts given by other people undergoing similar problems and yet the accounts are almost identical, even down to very subtle points within the investigation.

Surely this must give a person with an open mind, an indication that there is food for thought here and not just always the imagination of the misguided.

Some apparitional cases seem to go along with poltergeist-type activity therefore classifying cases is not particularly easy as often they cannot be placed into one particular 'slot.'

Chapter 3

POLTERGEIST ACTIVITY

'When science begins the study of non-physical phenomena, it will make more progress in one decade than in all the centuries of its experience'

DR FRED HOYLE, BRITISH COSMOLOGIST

Cases of the poltergeist type have been reported from antiquity occurring in all parts of the world. They are events in which places, not necessarily dwelling houses, and people seem to be subjected to physical phenomena where even heavy objects are overturned or displaced suddenly and inexplicably. Raps and bangs, some of which are so loud they could well have been made by a sledgehammer, are heard. Mysterious fires can break out, pools of water can appear, and people can be thrown out of bed. In modern cases electronic equipment often suffers inexplicable breakdowns. Often it would seem that the cause, whatever it is, results in an orgy of smashing or damaging any breakable objects such as crockery or window panes. In other cases, although it appears to the unfortunate people terrified by the variety of physical events that there is some mischievous, even malevolent, entity operating in repeated attempts to torment them, little or no damage to objects is seen almost as if care is being taken not to damage property. In some cases care also seems to be taken to avoid injuring any one seriously in spite of the fact that if they were struck by any of the sometimes heavy objects projected at speed, serious injury or even death would result. In a number of cases it is also reported that some form of response from the poltergeist to questions from the family or investigators may be set up using the old 'one rap for Yes, two raps for No' routine. Sometimes a case where physical phenomena happen can also include other phenomena such as apparitions or mysterious lights.

The reactions of visitors to the house involved can be stereotyped. Police, good psychical researchers and journalists, naturally strive to seek a normal explanation. Police have a reputation to maintain for solving crimes and so there is a tendency, whatever the evidence for paranormal events, no matter how many the witnesses, to look around for a culprit. If there are children in the house exhibiting stress and unhappiness which may be interpreted as hidden guilt, they can have pressure put upon them to confess to playing tricks. Care must be taken here as a child can be the focus for activity although they are not deliberately playing any trick or are even aware that they are the cause of the events. A later illustration may clarify this for you.

The word 'poltergeist' is German in origin and simply means 'noisy spirit'. To give it as an explanation of all cases classified as poltergeist cases begs the question for there are numerous cases, usually of comparatively short duration, that have been satisfactorily explained without invoking the theory that discarnate spirits were acting in them.

In this and the following chapters I give accounts of a number of cases, mostly modern cases, the majority being carefully investigated and studied by competent psychical researchers who were prepared to spend the necessary duration of time to do a proper job on them. Comparative studies of such cases enable a variety of conclusions to be drawn from them. By their existence, they challenge our model of scientific paradigms as surely, you might think, they now have no place in our modern scientific, educated age, but even today such cases occur. They demonstrate that they require and deserve careful study not only to enable investigators to help and support the unfortunate families and individuals caught up in the poltergeist torment but also to learn what they mean with respect to human personality and in some cases its possible survival of bodily death. They also seem to demonstrate beyond a reasonable shadow of doubt that mind, incarnate or discarnate, can move matter even over considerable distances, controlling it with amazing and mysterious dexterity.

Reid Kerr College Case

The following account is a case investigated by myself. In 1996 I was contacted by Mr Alan Carstairs who, at that time, was an arts teacher in a further education college in Renfrewshire. He was puzzled by various strange occurrences at the college, and indicated that he would like to discuss the unusual events with a hope that together they could perhaps make some kind of sense out of the situations.

He was the head of the pottery department and as such held a key to that section of the college, the only other key being held by the cleaner in order that she could tidy up of an evening and some mornings before classes started. The pottery accommodation consisted of two rooms, one at a higher level than the other - the upper level was the preparation area and the lower level housed the potter's wheel, clay, kiln etc.

One morning Alan arrived early to prepare for his classes and as he opened the door of the pottery section he saw three large pots which held glazing material in them, each about two and a half feet tall, on top of the large table on which the students worked in the upper pottery workspace. This table was about the size of a full sized table tennis table. The pots in question were normally located on the floor near the external door. Several unglazed items of pottery fashioned by students had been laid out on this table in a specific order, in fact in exactly the same order that Alan himself would have used, in preparation for the glazing of the aforesaid items. This in itself was strange, but even stranger was the fact that each of the pots on top of the table was nearly full of liquid glazing material. This in effect meant that, because of the combined weight of each pot and its liquid, it would have required at least three men to lift it. The fact that not one drop of glazing material had been spilled impressed Alan. It took three men a long time and a lot of effort to lift these pots down, and even while being very careful they usually spilled some of the liquid in the process.

It had been noted for some time, before this event, that items appeared to be going missing from locked cupboards and drawers within the two pottery workspaces. Only two head teachers had the keys for these cupboards and drawers, yet sometimes when they were opened, items were missing. They thought it odd but did not pursue the matter, and probably they secretly blamed each other. About the same time, the women cleaners were getting an uneasy feeling while they were cleaning an adjoining corridor to the pottery; both felt as though someone was watching them. They did not mention this to each other for fear of being thought stupid by the other person. On one particular day, one of the cleaners was left alone to finish the work, and as she was nearing the end of the aforesaid corridor she heard whispering which sounded to her as if it was coming from the janitor's room, which was just off this corridor. She actually thought to herself, quote, "That bugger's trying to frighten me, I'll teach him a lesson." and moved silently to the appropriate door of the janitor's room with the intention of scaring him. She flung open the door; there was no one inside and no other door existed in that room. Her response was to leave quickly.

Another evening, about five o'clock, the two cleaners were cleaning this same corridor and they decided to have a quick cup of tea in the kitchen which was about half way along this same corridor. They were enjoying their tea and a cigarette when they heard the sound of the door opening at the bottom of the corridor. This door had definitely been locked. They then heard the sound of heavy footsteps treading up the corridor towards their location. They could not imagine who it could be, and still the steps kept treading firmly and slowly towards them until the sound of them finally stopped completely outside the kitchen door. After tentatively saying "Who's there" and receiving no reply, one boldly opened the door to discover that there was no one there. No footsteps were heard going away from the door or treading along the corridor. No one could have disappeared as quickly as that. One woman got such a fright that she jumped onto the other one's lap and threw her arms around her neck (she felt very foolish about this later on). All tea drinking was suspended and in a highly emotional state they quickly checked all the appropriate doors to make sure that they were secure and then speedily left the building via the external door. On another occasion, Alan had remained behind after all the students had left as he was going to throw a very large pot using the potter's wheel. As previously mentioned this was in the lower section of the pottery. He then enlisted the help of a college labourer as the work was going to be quite cumbersome. In order that they would have privacy to do this they locked all of the external access doors, leaving the door to the lower pottery slightly ajar. They were doing well with the preparation of this large pot and were at a crucial point, where the labourer was bearing most of the weight while Alan fashioned the shape, when they heard the sound of an external door opening and the tread of footsteps on the two stone stairs, which are located just inside that door. This was followed by the sound of fairly solid footsteps on the wooden floorboards that cover the rest of that floor, coming towards the lower pottery. Alan was irritated by the interruption and muttered to the labourer "See who that is" although he really couldn't understand who it could be and probably didn't really care. The man stretched his head around the door to see who it was and to his surprise he found that there was no one there. This happened three times altogether while they were working with this pot, within roughly one hour. I have confirmatory testimony from the labourer that this was the case. No sounds were heard of the steps being retraced on any of the occasions. It should be noted that the door which sounded as though it was opening before the "footsteps" hit the two stone stairs was the same door described in the account of the cleaners in the corridor. When the two men had completed their work they checked all external and access doors and found them still to be locked.

Although of course it is not conclusive, both parties thought, due to the sound of the tread, that the footsteps were that of a man rather than a woman. The next noted event occurred during a winter period, when the weather was pretty cold outside and Alan was teaching a class in the lower pottery. The kilns, located in the lower pottery, had been on for some time as the class was preparing their work for firing. As a calor gas heater had also been on all day in this area it meant that the room was very warm indeed, somewhere in the order of thirty degrees. The work then complete, the class finished and was dismissed about 4.30pm. One of the mature students chose to wait for Alan while he retrieved his coat and jacket from the cloakroom, just outside the upper pottery area. The class having been dismissed and the calor fire and ovens closed down, everyone had left the lower pottery room and the door into it was closed. The mature student was therefore waiting in the upper room for Alan to return when he suddenly heard rattling and banging noises, which sounded as though they were coming from behind the lower pottery door. It was as if someone was locked in the lower pottery and was banging the door to get out. Just then Alan returned to hear the student yelling "You must have locked someone in there". Alan was puzzled as the lower room only required a turn of the handle to open the door from the other side. However he opened the door from the upper side with his key and was met with a blast of icy cold air that came rushing out of the room and across their faces, with almost a wooshing sound. Startled by this, they stepped down into the room out of curiosity and to their surprise found that no one was there and it was like walking into a chilled winter's night. The room was icy cold. The student left forthwith. As there had only been a time lapse of 4 minutes since the door was first closed, at the very most, this rapid change in temperature was again inexplicable.

Other more minor occurrences took place throughout the years. Curiously, after an old church pew was removed from the long corridor, which was adjacent to a lot of the phenomena locations, all of the strange activity seemed to cease. As there was no way of researching the history of this pew we cannot come to any conclusion about its possible relevance. It could have well been coincidence.

The teacher is as bemused by all of these happenings today as at the time. Nothing like this has ever happened to him or any of the other witnesses before or after these events.

In many spontaneous cases one effect that the experience appears to have on each recipient of the experience is noticeable. No matter the length of time after an inexplicable and impressive ostensible paranormal event has been witnessed, the memory of it does not swiftly decrease in clarity, unlike day to day happenings, that one might recall vaguely even a few days later. If I asked you to remember what you had for lunch three days ago, you would have to really think about it. The 'experiencer' remembers the intricate details of a paranormal event with crystal clear clarity, even many years later. The investigator must always attempt, by careful questioning of witnesses, to obtain a clear and accurate picture of the events.

Having visited the location several times and interviewed all of the witnesses individually, both on the premises and in their own homes, I have come to the conclusion that these people were telling me the truth, certainly as they saw it. But how (by what means) these events occurred, and the reason for them remains a mystery.

Electrical disturbances in spontaneous cases

Many cases that come to the attention of psychical researchers involve electrical appliances switching themselves on or off. A single example of this is in the next case involving the operation of the CD player, but there are numerous cases in which some form of electrical anomaly is reported in the form of electric kettles, toasters, televisions, lifts, video recorders and even washing machines switching on or off without a human agent being responsible in any normal way. Discounting fraud, no psychical researcher can honestly say that they know how this is done; only that it happens.

The Baker's Family

One evening during the summer of 1998, I received a telephone call from a very upset lady, whom I had never met. She sounded very anxious and worried as she told me of events which had recently occurred in her home; in fact she had trouble catching her breath while she was speaking to me. In this agitated condition she informed me that her family consisted of herself, her husband and their 18 year-old daughter.

Her husband was a baker and because of this their family routine was rather different from that of the average family in as much as meal times tended to be different to the norm in order that they could accommodate his shift patterns.

About 10.30pm on the Monday evening prior to this phone call, when everyone was in their respective beds, the mother and father heard the sound of music coming from their daughter's room. As this was not a usual occurrence, the mother went through to the daughter's room to investigate. The girl was sound asleep in her bed and the CD player was playing in her room. They thought it unusual as this was not something that the daughter normally did but did not think too much about it, maybe a power surge or something. The next day, Tuesday, actually 1.30am on Wednesday, again the parents were awakened by the sound of music coming from the girl's bedroom. They both went through and heard the strains of Elvis Presley singing "The wonder of you," and the music was again coming from the CD player while their daughter was sprawled over the bed, obviously fast asleep. On this occasion they really did think that this was unusual and very strange as there was no CD of Elvis singing "the wonder of you" in the machine, or even in the house.

The parents did not tell the girl of the events.

Wednesday afternoon saw the daughter sitting in the lounge reading a book while mother prepared the evening meal. Suddenly the sound of loud music was again heard, seemingly coming from upstairs. They remembered later, upon questioning, that it was classical music, but could not identify the piece. Both mother and daughter ran upstairs and stared at the CD player which was obviously the source of the music and then they stared at each other, as the CD player was not even plugged into the wall and that model of player has no battery facility.

Now the household was getting worried.

The next day, Thursday, the mother telephoned me. I listened sympathetically and suggested to her that there is usually a reason for these events, a change of some kind. Through questioning, I tried to ascertain information that might shed some light on the happenings. Despite my questioning she maintained that nothing unusual had happened in the family, the family was not under stress of any kind, no one had changed job, no one stressed by exams and that no one in their group of family and friends was extremely ill or had died. None of this was making any sense to me as, through experience of this type of phenomenon I knew that there had to be a reason if the account was a true one. Experience has shown that there is always a trigger of some kind before events of this kind occur. Finding the motivation, cause or the stimulus is often the difficult part. Along with many other things in life, once you identify the reason, you can then hopefully do something about a problem. After further probing, it transpired in conversation that Tom, a close friend of the family, had recently died in Leeds. She had not mentioned this to me before because she had not thought that it could be important.

Tom and her husband had been great friends and avid football fans. Tom was a Rangers supporter whereas her husband, the baker, was a fanatical Celtic supporter and the two men always used to exchange banter over their differences in a good natured and humorous fashion, when the friend was alive and well. It seemed to them that Tom appeared to change in personality when he discovered that he was dying of cancer and during his term of illness there was a 'bite' in the exchange of football opinions. Tom said to them in a fairly nasty way that he would come back and haunt this family after he had "gone". I think that subconsciously the mother and father were a bit afraid of this.

When I asked the time of Tom's death I was told that he had passed last Monday; you may remember that the phenomena began on Monday evening. The funeral was to be the next day, Friday, after this phone call to me. It was being held in Leeds.

I asked her if Tom was a bit of a joker and the life and soul of the party when he was alive and well and she replied that indeed he was. I pointed out that all of the music played "paranormally" was pleasant and no harm seemed to be intended, to which she agreed. I postulated the idea that perhaps Tom was possibly merely drawing their attention to the fact that in some way his intelligence had survived and wanted to let them know that he was all right. Possibly indicating "look I've made it"

As she had told me that the funeral was to be the next day following our conversation I ventured the opinion that there was a possibility that after the funeral they may hear no more about him, but of course could not guarantee this. Once we had discussed these things for a time the lady seemed a lot less tense and appeared to agree that my suggestion followed certain logic. As we normally do, I gave her the freedom to call me back if there were any more strange occurrences and we could investigate the matter further.

Since that day I have heard nothing concerning any further events. I can only conclude that all was peaceful and quiet from then on.

The Conservatory

A few years ago I drove Professor Archie Roy about sixty miles to a case location to visit a family apparently very upset by the paranormal phenomena taking place in their home. The husband was a college lecturer, the lady worked in a semi-professional occupation and the home was a very comfortable one in every way.

Before arriving at this site we had not been told about the scale of phenomena allegedly taking place, but could appreciate the extent to which the people were affected by the nervous manner in which the telephone call was made when they asked for our help.

The house was absolutely pristine inside and out and the man and woman were extremely friendly; both appeared to be quiet and conservative in nature. After some time in their company we established the following.

They had a conservatory built over the previous six months and one Sunday afternoon, shortly after the basic structure of the conservatory had been erected, they noted a strong smell of tobacco smoke within it. This was very odd as smoking was not permitted within this house, there were no close neighbours and no one smoked. A short time later, the daughter of this family had made an appointment for a hairdresser to come around to cut and colour her hair and they were going to use the incomplete conservatory as a salon, no doubt to minimise dirtying the house. Five people in all ended up in the conservatory when the hairdresser arrived.

About half way through the hairdressing procedure everyone in the room remarked that they could smell strong tobacco smoke, like that from an old pipe. It was quite a pungent unmistakable aroma.

No one thought too much of it, merely that it was curious. After the structure of the conservatory was complete, that is when the walls were finished, outside and inside, windows were in place, internal plaster work complete and decoration was about to commence, the husband in particular noticed that every time he came into the conservatory that one of the windows was open. He was absolutely certain on each occasion that he had closed it and thought that perhaps someone else had reopened it. He asked his wife and daughter, several times, if they had opened the window but they stated emphatically that they had not. This was really annoying him now as he thought that the workmen had not done their job properly and perhaps the catches were faulty, so to test this theory he thought that he would conduct an experiment. Having made sure that all the windows were closed properly and while he was he only person in the house, he went upstairs to do something and when he came down again one window was open. He closed this window and then taped up all of the windows with heavy masking tape and when he next returned all of the windows were shut just as he had left them, but the back door was wide open.

For a time he did not tell his wife about this happening since she was already nervous enough over the previous sensation of the smell of smoke in the conservatory.

Things then began to escalate. Upon their return, after all were out for an evening, they entered the lounge to find that all of the framed pictures had been taken off the walls and laid in a row, with great precision, up the middle of the lounge floor on top of the carpet. Not one of the cords that had held the pictures on to the hooks had been broken, and no hooks were damaged either. The pictures were easily replaced in their original positions.

They were now becoming really anxious.

When they had been out another evening they returned to find that all of the light bulbs had been taken out of the lounge lamps and were lying neatly arranged in a line, once again, on the lounge carpet. Not one bulb was broken and all of them could be relocated and reused. On yet another evening upon their return, the light overlooking the fish tank was switched off at the wall but the power switch to the mechanism controlling the water temperature was untouched and the tropical fish were unhurt. The location of this light switch, beside the power switch, was very awkward to reach, both being behind and under the fish tank level on the wall, which precluded any accidental hitting of the switch by any person at an earlier point in the day.

While the decoration of the conservatory was progressing, two or three shelves had been erected on one of the walls; the highest of these being about 8 feet from floor level and a few ornaments had been placed on these shelves.

One day a neighbour, another lecturer, called to visit the husband to view and admire the progress of the new conservatory. While they were talking and looking around, the house owner pointed up towards a shelf on which was displayed a heavy straw model of a Viking ship. As they looked up, one of the straw paddles very slowly detached itself from the vessel, rose up about two inches and travelled half way across the room horizontally before it gently floated to the floor in a deliberate zig-zag manner. Even a feather would have travelled faster. The men looked directly into each other's eyes; the neighbour took to his heels and hastened homewards. We cannot say what happened after that but up until the time of our visit he had never returned to visit this couple again.

The final event, the clincher as it were, before they called for help occurred when the lady of the house opened a walk-in cupboard door, entered, and a light bulb came out of its holder and dropped on her head, giving her quite a bit of discomfort. The lady's hysterical reaction to this seemed to convince them ask for our assistance.

Through questioning we established that they had a very good friend called David, who over a period of years, used to visit them regularly. The lady of this house, as previously indicated, was very house-proud and she would not allow anyone to smoke inside the house. This became a regular topic of conversation every time David called, due to the fact that he was a pipe smoker. Each time he wanted to smoke his pipe he had to go outside of the house to do so. Some months before the couple started the building of the extension to their home the lady had made a promise to David that he could smoke his pipe in this extension, conservatory, when it was finished. Sadly, David took ill and died before this addition to the house was complete.

On reflection the couple agreed that the smell of pipe tobacco was similar to that used by the deceased David.

After listening to the reports of the happenings already described in this chapter, it seemed at least a possibility that David was trying to tell the couple that he was aware of them in some way and could interact with their lives. An alternative 'normal' explanation is that the couple were telling lies and making up the whole story. This alternative became increasingly highly improbable as we learned more and more about the couple.

If you could have seen the effect that the events had on these people you would know that they were not telling deliberate lies. The lady in particular had a fairly rigid belief system and would not take on board that these things were actually occurring, although she knew that they were. She would only admit the strange happenings to herself after she was hit on the head by the light bulb.

It was an interesting fact of the phenomena that the items displayed on the lounge carpet were neatly laid out, almost reflecting the neatness of the lady of the house.

After many hours of talking with, and listening to, the couple, the husband could follow a logical train of thought to the possible conclusion that in some way David could be responsible for the strange events and could understand why he may have become a little "upset" when no-one would recognise that he had come to visit. It seems just like a close friend coming to visit and having the door shut in their face. The suggestion that it could be David who was responsible for the events did not sit well with the lady as she, almost hysterically, just kept saying "But he shouldn't be here, he shouldn't be here!"

We asked them, within themselves, to wish David well, wherever he may be and to think nothing but pleasant thoughts about him. They agreed to try this. By the time we left, the man had a more placid attitude to the whole affair. When we departed they were not nearly so stressed as they were upon our arrival, hopefully because intelligent people had taken them seriously and were trying to understand and possibly make sense of their problem.

Sometimes people imagine that some sort of demon is about to appear through the walls and capture or injure them. This is probably the fault of popular media productions, movies and shock-horror reporting, in the search for sensationalism and viewing figures.

One thing that we have come to accept is that there is always a reason behind the production of phenomena; once you have pinpointed a possible reason, whether it is on-going or historical, incarnate or discarnate in source, then you can begin to look towards a possible resolution, or at least some kind of understanding.

Once again, we have had no further word from the people involved in this case. We can only assume that all is well and that no further activities occurred, or that the phenomena have settled down to an acceptable level that can be tolerated by the couple, or the phenomena have ceased since the departed had now been recognised by the couple.

New House

Five or six years ago, I was invited to investigate strange activity in a newly built house which stood on a luxury estate in Lanarkshire. The inhabitants were a pleasant young couple who lived there with their five-month-old baby. The only information that we had been given before going to the location was that strange "things" were reported to be happening in the home, but in no detail.

The house had been built on land that had had no previous housing on it, at least during the last two hundred years or so, and the couple had lived there for about two years without experiencing any problems at all.

I took Professor Archie Roy along with me. The couple seemed very tense initially when we arrived and were even reticent to tell us of the recent strange events. Eventually the first account was given of the evening, when they had been watching television and the baby was fast asleep in his cot upstairs, they heard a sound akin to that of a mechanical winding mechanism, coming from a part of the room that had a small recess. As they looked towards the source of the sound, they saw two of the mechanical toys, which had been sitting on the floor in that recess come towards them. They watched open mouthed, in disbelief, as the toys moved across the floor towards them. Both of them knew that the toys had been there, unattended, for hours. After the initial shock and disbelief they stared at each other in silence while exhibiting amazed looks. Nothing was said to the other.

Another evening, a day or so later within the same scenario, a helium balloon at the top of a long string, which was located in this same secluded recess of the lounge, began whirling around in a circular motion. As both parents watched, it appeared to gain momentum as it moved and as they looked at it they both saw a pulsating blue-white light above the balloon that seemed to increase in intensity with each gyration. The two adults observed this for what seemed like several minutes. The husband's reaction was to run up the internal stairs to the bedroom, jump into bed and pull the covers over his head. When I asked him about this he sheepishly agreed that was his course of action.

The balloon was in such a position in the recess of the lounge that the location precluded any chance of it being blown by a draught of any description. We tested for this upon our visit. There were no doors or windows in this recess and it was not subject to any draught from any other source.

As is our protocol, we questioned the people separately and their accounts of the events were identical.

Over the previous months they had individually noticed several odd things happening about the house but had not said anything to each other, as there was nothing definite in their minds to tell. Both had experienced the feeling that they were being watched in some sense, but dismissed the thought as imagination, and as previously stated had not mentioned it to each other. Neighbours reported to the couple that they could see someone sitting on their settee, as if watching TV, while the couple were out of the home and the neighbours just naturally assumed that they had a visitor or visitors. On a fairly regular basis, some items in the home were not in the same place as they had been left when they returned of an evening. We can all forget things and make errors of judgement but they were certain of these changes. A favourite piece selected for relocation was a vase situated in the hall display unit. Each night upon their return, they would put it back into the display cabinet in the hall and each evening when they came back home it had been moved to another room. This was said to have happened many times along with other items, but this was the favourite. The house had an internal staircase and sometimes the baby was seen to be looking up the stairs and smiling at "something" at the top of the stairs.

The husband and wife were now becoming perplexed and had to admit that they were frightened as they wondered what on earth was going to happen next. All in all the couple were none too happy. At this point they wondered vaguely that it might be something to do with the ground on which the house was built.

Upon further questioning it transpired that the girl's mother had died not long before their baby was born and also that the girl was suffering a little from post-natal depression. This was not surprising under the circumstances, with her mother dying just before the birth of her baby.

As there was no obvious intent to harm anyone in the home and they had lived quite happily in this location for two years previously, we began to wonder if it was possible that the girl's mother, in some sense, had anything to do with this. I asked the husband if his mother-in-law was an interfering type of person when she was alive and the answer was most definitely affirmative. My reply was to the effect that she may still be taking an interest in the family. The husband was silent for a moment or two and looked very thoughtful before uttering "Can you not make her go away?" (I have moderated his actual response)

His wife did not look too amused at his response but she did look much happier in general and had better skin colour and tone than she had upon our arrival. It seemed that this positive change could be attributed to the thought that her mother may be around in some way to help and take an interest in all of them. This also visibly changed her total appearance. As a matter of interest the vase in the hall which was repeatedly being moved was a present from her mother.

Unfinished business often seems to be a factor in various types of paranormal phenomena. It seems reasonable to think that a mother, whose life was cut short, could be trying to make her influence known, just as she would if she were alive. If some sort of survival occurs what could be more natural than that the lady would want to see her grandchild and help her daughter at this time, especially if she was feeling low with post natal depression.

After discussion with the couple it was decided to leave the situation as it was, with the suggestion that when the girl was strong enough to cope with life on her own, the mother may move "on" of her own accord. The husband was not entirely happy with this but he could see the sense in it and we did give him the option of phoning us at anytime if the circumstances changed in any way, with the promise that we could return, possibly with a sensitive, and look further into the situation.

To date we have heard no more about this case and that is now over six years ago. When we left that household everyone was smiling, unlike the drawn scared faces of the inhabitants when we arrived.

The following case is an example of parsimony from a departed person.

Cardigan

I heard of this case from a lady on the staff of Glasgow University. Her mother and father had retired and bought a little dream cottage set in rural surroundings in a very pleasant situation in the north of Scotland. Although idyllic in some sense there was only one open fire in the cottage which meant that the bedroom was much colder than the living room. Because of this the gentleman was in the habit of undressing for bed and changing into his pyjamas in the lounge, in front of the fire. He would place his clothes either over or on a chair in the lounge. One evening, after taking off his heavy duty cable knit cardigan, he draped it over the back of a chair in the usual manner before retiring to bed. This cardigan had 6 round leather buttons. The next morning when he went to put on the cardigan he noticed that two of the buttons were missing. He was puzzled by this as he was sure that they had been there the previous night, but his wife blamed him (as we ladies do) for losing them and being careless. As she happened to have a couple of identical spare buttons she sewed them on to replace the missing ones.

That evening he, once again, draped the cardigan over the aforesaid chair. The next morning it was found that three buttons were missing from the cardigan. His wife once again laid the blame at his feet and made it known that she was none too pleased. She then made a journey to shops, a fair distance away, especially to purchase a new set of buttons, which she duly sewed on to the cardigan on her return to the cottage. That evening when the cardigan was draped yet again over the chair, the lady of the house examined the said cardigan thoroughly before both parties trooped off to bed. When they came through to the lounge the next morning the cardigan had no buttons on it at all!

Upon questioning the lady who gave the account, she told me that her sister had tragically died quite recently. I asked her about her sister's character and she laughed and said that she was quite a joker. She also agreed that the button situation was just something that she might have done. And so it would appear that this lady could make herself known to her mother and father not terribly long after her death.

Incidentally, the buttons were never found.

Once again we appear to have an example of someone who just wanted to be recognised or perhaps to say 'I've made it'.

Chapter 4

HYBRID CASES – APPARITIONS WITH POLTERGEIST PHENOMENA

Just as occurs in illnesses, where a patient may be found to be suffering from two or more different sources of his symptoms, which makes the illness difficult to identify and treat, cases of psychic phenomena may be of multiple origin. The question sometimes arises: is the patient the house, does it act like a person who has been exposed to an infection, or infections? Does the house behave like the object - a letter in a sealed envelope, or some small personal belonging – which, when picked up by a psychic, enables the psychic to experience events related to the object's previous owner? Or is it in some way the house's previous inhabitant, now deceased, still present in the house as an 'earthbound'? Is there more than one previous inhabitant still around?

I now give a number of such cases, where dwellings seem to possess 'residues', in one form or another, of former occupants.

The Shanter Inn

A location which has long been linked with the Scottish Society for Psychical Research began its association with us around 1994 when

Professor Archie Roy and I were asked to visit "The Shanter Inn" located in the little town of Kirkoswald in Ayrshire, Scotland. Strange and ghostly events were reported to be happening at this hotel.

At first, to be honest, we were suspicious that the request for us to visit might be a publicity stunt by the owners of that time, and so we travelled down incognito as it were to that location one Saturday at lunchtime in order that we could quietly assess the situation.

We ordered lunch and made a visual scan of the premises. The lunch was very good indeed, the hotel was most pleasant and all of the staff seemed very friendly. We were seated at our lunch table and I had briefly noted at my back a small bay window as I took my seat. It was a beautiful day and very warm, the temperature must have been nearly thirty degrees Celsius outside; all in all everything was very pleasant. Every so often, while we were eating and talking, I felt as though my hair was being touched quite lightly at the back of my head. I assumed that it was a tassel from a roller blind or the leaf of a pot plant that was intermittently being blown by a breeze causing me to feel this touch, and I did not pay too much attention to it as we were engrossed in conversation (and eating).

Towards the end of the meal, Archie left the table and I took the opportunity to turn around to see what was catching the back of my head. I was immediately puzzled as there was nothing there at all, and I do mean nothing, just a flat window ledge going from behind my shoulder level, back to the furthest point about eighteen inches away, where it met the window. Like most human beings I said nothing about this, as I did not know Professor Roy very well at that time and I did not want to be thought of as an idiot with a vivid imagination.

After lunch we introduced ourselves to the owners Eric and Celia and invited them to tell us of their experiences regarding the reported strange occurrences. They told us that one morning, a few days earlier, Celia had walked into the hotel kitchen (in good daylight) to find a small man seated on a ledge to the right of the kitchen door. He was swinging his legs to and fro, as they were too short to reach the floor. He gave her a huge smile and she smiled back while trying to think who he could be and how he came to be there. All at once he disappeared (in her words) through the wall, right in front of her eyes. She was flabbergasted. When relating her experience, she appeared to be most genuine and simply puzzled and curious about the experience. The man was described as short in height, having a round, reddish face, wearing a waistcoat type of jacket, an apron and something like a cravat around his neck.

After a lengthy briefing that put us in the picture, we investigated the premises and I must say that the first floor corridor did have a strange "feel" about it, sort of strangely cool and it made the hair on one's arms "stand up" in an electrostatic manner.

After looking around the other sections of the hotel, we went downstairs to the main lounge for a further talk and a cup of tea. I ask you to remember that it was a really hot day. About an hour or so into further conversation I began to feel incredibly chilled, as if from the inside outwards; I could not shake this sensation as it felt most unpleasant and I felt quite unwell. By this time we had been at least three hours all told at the Inn. After signalling to Archie that we should go, we made our way through the car park and before I could say anything Archie said to me "I feel incredibly chilled." As he looked at me he must have wondered why I was smiling; I told him of course. It took the two of us about two hours to recover, thaw out, and feel at all normal.

There were no lasting effects, but it was very strange that we should both react in the same way from an apparently unconscious level, as the physical room temperature was certainly over seventy degrees Fahrenheit.

Unbeknown to Professor Roy and I at this time was the fact that many people in the past had reported a feeling of "chill" in the downstairs bar, especially near the inner door to the lounge, in fact it was quite a tangible feeling, as if walking into invisible cold smoke. This resulted in them feeling shivers running up and down their backs. And that was before they had a drink!

Other purported happenings included a report from one of the hotel staff, Charlotte. One day she was in the process of changing the bed linen in a twin room, the beds being parallel to each other between two opposite walls. She had completed restoring covers and pillows to one bed and walked across the quite small room to make up the other bed, which she did. When she had completed the task she then turned around in the usual manner to check her handiwork, she observed the shape of a body under the covers of the first bed which she had just made. This shape was of full human size and had embossed the covers to just the correct height were a real person really underneath the covers. No one could have come into the room as she was working beside the only entrance to that room. Charlotte was terrified; she ran screaming from the room and was afraid to go back in again. In actual fact, even a year later she would not close the door of that room while doing any chores no matter how simple or how quickly they could be done; such was her fear.

Many people in the downstairs bar, on several occasions, have heard footsteps treading up the internal stairs and walking along the first floor corridor; in fact when they were first aware of it people used to rush up the stairs to try to catch the "intruder", but there was never anyone there. All of this transpired of course at a time when no one was legitimately or otherwise on that first floor for any reason whatsoever.

We decided to call back another time and bring a "sensitive" with us, someone who could perhaps pick up impressions of the hotel and surroundings, and shed some light on the matter.

Just as a point of interest, the hotel lounge, including the bar area itself, incorporates part of the old school which Robert Burns, the poet, attended in the 18th century. Across the road from the hotel is a graveyard where the bodies of several people who were inspirational as role models for some of Burns' characters are buried, among them being Souter Johnny ; the gravestones may be viewed and are quite attractive as some of them have three-dimensional illustrations on them.

There is no doubt about it; the layout of the whole area is very atmospheric.

The medium who accompanied us to the Shanter Inn was none other than the now deceased Albert Best. No pun is intended but Albert was recognised by all as one of the best mediums in this country and abroad. We did not tell him where we were going nor did we describe any of the reported phenomena, in fact we really did not tell him anything at all other than we were going to a location where phenomena had been reported. I have to say that he did grumble a bit as we passed the first hour of our journey time, but that was our Albert. Upon arrival at the hotel and after a cup of tea, we gave him a free hand to wander around the premises in the hope that he might pick up "something" with his extrasensory talent. He sensed that there had been a fire at one time on the first floor, however these owners were not in a position to confirm or deny this statement.

When he went into the yard he was aware of a man walking across it carrying two leather buckets, one in each hand. He described the man as smallish, having a round tummy, a jovial face with ruddy cheeks and wearing a kerchief type of material around his neck and a leather apron around his waist. This description may sound familiar to you as it is almost identical to the one given by the proprietor earlier in this account. Albert had a "word" with him and tried to persuade him to leave the premises as it were, since he should not really be there, but was told in reply, much to Albert's chagrin, that he was quite happy where he was and was not willing to go anywhere else. Even after further attempts at persuasion he was quite determined that he was happy where he was and refused to budge. I have to say that Albert was a bit annoyed by this and kept repeating "but he shouldn't be here, he shouldn't be here."

About two years later, the Shanter Inn changed hands and the new owners, especially the gentleman, did not believe a word of any of the accounts of any strange events which were reported in the past, dismissing them as nonsense. That is until one evening at 11pm, I received a telephone call from that very upset gentleman to tell me of an event that had just happened to him when he was alone in the house and while he was taking a shower. He heard his name being called, twice, and stopped the shower, wrapped himself in a towel and went to see who it was. No one was there. When he returned to complete his shower the water was running and he is certain that he turned it off. Let me just say that after that he was not so sceptical. It's like everything else in life; if a person has a particular experience they *know* that they have had that experience, nothing will alter their opinion, but if you have not had that particular experience, then how can you judge it? Some time after this his grown up daughter, while sleeping in her bed, awakened in the wee small hours to hear footsteps coming down the two stairs at the entrance to her bedroom, she heard the floorboards creaking and was now by this time wide awake and round eyed. As she looked up a figure of a man appeared at the foot of her bed. She noted that his feet did not touch the floor - as he had no feet, and in some way he seemed to be self - illuminated. She threw her arm out to try to switch on her bedside lamp and scattered the lamp onto the floor, where it shattered into many pieces. For months after this, she kept breaking bedside lamps and destroyed at least five of them over this time every time she heard even a natural creak. Eventually she adopted the habit of sleeping with a light on all night.

Subsequent to our visit, many years later after the original investigation, a group of trainee psychical researchers for the Scottish Society for Psychical Research, visited this hotel and executed an all-night vigil. There were 12 of them. Each felt the peculiar atmosphere in the first floor corridor. A person, who was standing vigil in this corridor, also felt that something touched him on the shoulder, not just a gentle touch but with a light pressure applied. Another saw a type of mist, at a different time, in this same corridor, and two others heard a loud bang, for which they could not account, coming from near a fireplace at the far end of the downstairs lounge. They examined all of the logical possibilities and could not find a satisfactory, or even a probable, answer. As far as we were aware, the "gentleman" was still there and the mystery continued.

In September of 2002 I had a call from the proprietor to say that two ladies had complained to him about the constant banging noise within their bedroom on the previous evening. They described the sound as rhythmic and coming from inside the room. This particular room had no other guest-room adjacent to it, no water pipes overhead or underneath, in fact no suitable explanation could be found to explain away the sounds. The ladies were very frightened by this experience. So much so that they wrote details of it down and gave it to the owner the next morning. These ladies were strangers who knew nothing of the past events in the Inn, and, yes, this room is part of the flat where the girl saw the illuminated figure.

Around October 2002, some guests were dining in the downstairs dining room in the Shanter when one of the diners looked up as something caught his eye to see a man "walk" through the wall facing him. He was the only one of his party to be facing in that direction at that time. On the other side of this wall, at this spot, is the kitchen ledge described by Celia, in the beginning of this account, where the man "disappeared." The diner told the proprietor of his experience later and was able to describe the man. It fitted the description given by Albert Best all those years before.

In 2005, Nick Kyle, a member of the SSPR, had a telephone call from the proprietor to say that workmen, who were due to stay over for a few nights, only stayed for one due to the unwarranted effects of "something strange."

Sadly in 2008, the Shanter Inn, as we knew it, had a major refurbish and is now owned by a chain of hotels. I wonder if we will be called in again in the future.

The House at Maxwell Park

It has been said that there are haunted places and haunted people and that cases can be conveniently placed in one or other of these classes. In the class of haunted people you often find poltergeist cases. In psychical research however, nothing is ever certain and some poltergeist cases seem to exhibit phenomena common to both classes from the movement of objects to the ostensible invasion of minds. Again, some poltergeist cases are mild in their phenomena and of short duration - a day or two. In others the phenomena are more severe and varied, running their course in a few weeks. Occasionally, as in the Enfield case, which will be the next case to be described, the phenomena escalate in variety, force and malevolence, tormenting the luckless family involved for a year or more. The Maxwell Park case was another case running over a period of time. It was investigated by the Rev. Max Magee and Archie. Roy. In the following account, by Roy, the names of everyone concerned in the case except for Magee's name and Roy's have been changed. The names used are therefore fictitious but the facts are as stated below.

There were three families involved, the Uppinghams, the Schwarzs and the Downies. Mr Walter Uppingham was aged about 45, his wife Mrs. Jean Uppingham was about 40, their two sons, Ian and David being about 14 and 11. Mrs Grant, about 70, the mother of Mrs Jean Uppingham, lived with them.

The second family consisted of Hugo Schwarz, a Dutchman of about 55 who fought in the Dutch resistance during the war. His wife Mavis was about 50 and a sister of Mrs Jean Uppingham, their daughter, Janet, about 19, suffered from a very severe speech and hearing impediment. Their two sons John and Peter were about 22 and 21 years of age.

The Uppinghams lived above the Downies, the third family. Mr Downie was about 65-70, his wife being about 65-70 while their son Frank was about 30 years of age.

By the time the case was in full swing, many other people had become involved, including the police, town councillors, family doctors and a psychiatrist, joiners, plumbers, electricians and the GPO, (the state telephone company), spiritualists, the parish minister, neighbours, newspaper reporters and sundry others.

The situation began about November 1974. The Uppinghams and the Downies had had a very serious confrontation to the extent that they now hated each other. If Mr Downie had said 'Good Morning' to Mr Uppingham, or vice versa, the other would have said, 'I wonder what that devil is getting up to now'. In other words they were totally beyond the reach of rationality as far as their quarrel was concerned. In particular the two boys, Ian and David, had had a feud with the grown-up son Frank Downie.

Mr & Mrs Downie were retired. At the time in question, Mr Downie had a very serious illness which ultimately proved fatal, and Frank himself had a history of illness.

The first phase of the occurrences lasted between 3rd November 1974 and the 4th December 1974. It involved tappings, bangings and scratching noises. The Uppinghains held the Downies responsible. There was also an incident of a Guy Fawkes bonfire on which the two boys had burned an effigy of Mr Downie. This did not help to spread sweetness and light.

The upstairs people got a bit tired of the rapping and banging and sent for the police. The police warned the Downies who said it was the people upstairs. The police said, 'well don't do it again' and went away. The banging continued, even when the police came back later and took the Downies to the police station

As the nights passed, the number of people involved grew until town councillors and police were upstairs and downstairs. The police downstairs thought the noises were coming from upstairs and the people upstairs thought the noises were coming from downstairs. On interviewing the Inspector in charge of the case, he told Roy that he had had to take one or two of his policemen off the case as they were turning in accounts that 'the bed was proceeding in a northerly direction'! At this stage, in fact, the town councillors and police had been joined by family doctors, joiners, plumbers, electricians and the GPO because a very thorough investigation was carried out to see whether any of these noises could be attributed to natural causes.

A further escalation occurred in which objects now began to fly across the room upstairs, according to the testimony of the Uppinghams, to such an extent that the Uppinghams fled to their relatives, the Schwarz's, who lived about three quarters of a mile away. And of course, in true poltergeist fashion, it, whatever it was, moved with them and set up house in the Schwarz's. This particular early phase from 3rd November 1974 to 4th December 1974 ended with a service conducted by a member of the Faculty of Divinity of Glasgow University, Professor Murdo Ewan Macdonald, assisted by the Rev. Max Magee. The service seemed to be successful.

The following is a statement by Mr Uppingham, written at the end of this first period when it was believed that the disturbances had died away.

'The following evening my wife attempted to put our two sons in our bed; she even lay beside them on top of our bed hoping to get some sleep or rest, no matter how little but this was not to be, not this night nor for many nights to come. Less than 5 minutes later a repeat performance of what took place in the boys' bedroom began again only this time our bedside table shuddered and everything fell on the floor including a table lamp, ash tray, glass paper weight and a small travel alarm clock. We then proceeded to the lounge. I tried to calm them down by telling them that probably the overhanging bedclothes had knocked the items off the table accidentally.

'We replaced everything. We tried to get some sleep again but no sooner had we settled down when once again a scream came from my bedroom. This time the table had shaken so violently that those same objects had now been thrown right across the room. My wife and I immediately retreated from the bedroom and after trying to calm our frayed nerves we decided to spend what remained of the night in sleeping bags on the lounge floor. We had to go through to our room again to collect the sleeping bags. As were doing this the bedside lamp flickered for a few seconds and then went out. I left the room thinking that the bulb had fused but a few moments later the light came on again. We discovered that our dog Rex seemed unable to settle in any room in the house. He usually slept peacefully in the boys' bedroom.

'Being a musician, my wife and our younger son David, who is also musical, recognized that the tappings were tapping out the Death March. My wife asked if this was a very sick practical joke. From then onwards we were aware that something rather unnatural was happening. The problem was how we could decipher these tappings.'

It occurred to them that they could use the age-old method of one rap for 'yes' two raps for 'no'. The result was that they seemingly got into contact with 'spirits' on the other side. The message which was received informed them of a pit disaster which happened in the immediate area many years before and resulted in the deaths of some miners. The 'spirits' went on to tell them that they could not find rest but wanted to find peace through the efforts of the family.

The banging then started again. I should say that at the height of these bangings the house would shake as if a sledgehammer was being used on the walls every 4 seconds. Pictures would come off the wall and fall back again. Furniture would shake. (Certainly the noises were objective for they were captured on a tape recorder).

The Uppinghams 'phoned for the police again. Mr Uppingham states:

'After explaining to the police what we had witnessed we were asked to put our sons to bed again and as expected the tapping began. Now we had new witnesses to our dilemma. Now the faces of doubt were being replaced by expressions of amazement and another sleepless night was spent.'

After a while they got in touch with a medium and a person simply described as a gentleman active in the field of psychic research. A séance was arranged and again they got the story of the miners who had died in the pit disaster. It is well-known that the whole area of Maxwell Park is honeycombed with old pit shafts. The Uppinghams then fled to their relatives' house and it was apparent, Mr Uppingham goes on, that their unwanted guest had followed them.

'We spent the remainder of that night sitting on a settee facing the fire. And to our astonishment we saw an ornamental model of a whiskey barrel made of wood and brass suddenly being thrown upwards and on to the floor. Within seconds of this happening a picture, built on a swivel, revolved to show the mirrored side and shortly afterwards a basket-work box turned a half-somersault before our eyes, to show us the base of the box.'

The next manifestation to take place while the entire family were in the lounge was equally astonishing. Mrs Uppingham was the first person to feel drops of water falling from the ceiling on to her arm. Her younger son also saw drops of water falling onto his trouser leg.

'The next people to share this experience with us were my sister-in-law and her younger son, who is 21. We examined the ceiling and found there was no justifiable reason why this should happen as the ceiling was perfectly dry and free from any condensation whatsoever.'

They then phoned the local priest who came along and blessed the house.

It was decided that Mr Uppingham's wife, their sons and his wife's nephew should spend the night in the lounge and this they did. They were all falling asleep in an upright position when MrsUppingham's nephew began to cough uncontrollably and thought he saw cigarette smoke drifting past him. At that moment her elder son began a fit of coughing, followed in turn by Mrs Uppingham. A heavy smoker's ashtray crashed to the floor beside them, then a large model of a Dutch windmill (a musical box) began to play. The sails turned round and a tea-trolley which supported the windmill was wheeled some 12 inches from where it stood. When they returned in despair to their own house, the Uppinghams found, according to their report, that the water taps were turned on to such an extent that it was impossible, without a wrench, to turn them off again, whereupon much of the house was flooded. They then got a plumber to come along and adjust them but the following day the same thing happened again.

'One of the Professors (sic) came along and held a service in our lounge while prayers were said by all. The other Professor (sic), the Rev. Max Magee, placed his hands on the heads of my sons and lastly myself. This he repeated once more. He then went into my sons' bedroom with them and told them to go to bed. He stayed with them until they fell asleep, and there were no noises at this time. There were other phenomena but after further service everything seemed quiet.'

The member of Glasgow University Faculty of Divinity stated that on 29th November 1974, he was contacted by Inspector Butler of the Eastern Division, Partick. He had been appointed as independent investigator into the unusual happenings. He goes on to give a summary of the situation.

'When I called I found the family, especially the parents, in a state bordering on hysteria. The strain showed visibly on their faces. The father was obsessed with the subject of the dead miners. He talked compulsively about the dead miner Tom Watson and he had even done some research in the Mitchell Library and had found that there had indeed been a 1929 mine disaster in that area. I suggested that the two boys should go to bed in the room where the noises originally occurred. On opening the bedroom door I was struck by the low temperature. It was like going into a refrigerator. As soon as the light was put out the tappings began. Some seemed to come from the head of the bed and others from the side walls. Mr Uppingham, convinced he was in touch with the miner Tom Watson, put a number of questions. In this manner he received an unequivocal answer to all the questions he put. During the evening I saw a door shut when no one was near. I also heard alarm clocks going off three or four times at random and in the kitchen I had a most uncanny and eerie feeling; the hair at the back of my neck bristled, I had a tingling feeling down my spine and two arms. Next morning Mr Uppingham 'phoned me at the University. Since my visit the manifestations had moved on to a different level. He had seen a standing ashtray move across the room. He had also seen a coffee table levitate and had to use both hands to put it down to the floor. Toys had been moved as well, one breaking a window and landing in the front garden. Mr Uppingham was polite, but I got the distinct impression that my visit had not helped.

'I held a service in the house. While I conducted the exorcism service, a reading (The Beatitudes, St. Matthew Chapter 5), a Prayer, in which I commanded whatever it was to go and leave the family in peace, the Rev. Max Magee laid hands in blessing on every member of the family. After the service the phenomena seemed to disappear.'

That was the end of the first phase. The second phase began on 6th January about a month later and lasted until 18th January. It began interestingly enough following a Nationwide TV programme on a similar case. In addition to noises and movements of articles there was now an increase in the number of what one might call anti-personnel movements, seemingly motivated by malice - scattering of toys, movements of beds. The Schwarz household was not as much involved as the Uppinghams. A medium came back again, concentrated on the miner disaster story, a séance was again held and all became quiet at the Uppinghams except that a certain amount of trouble continued at the Schwarz's especially when Ian went to stay there for a fortnight.
Mr Uppingham prepared a report on the second phase:

'Tonight the BBC TV program, Nationwide, interviewed tenants in Newcastle who occupied a block of council flats, where it seemed unexplainable noises were heard and objects were scattered about. After seeing that programme I took David to his music lesson. I decided to make a tape-recording of our story. This I started. I was only recording for about 15 minutes when there was a thump outside my bedroom door. I opened the door quickly and at the same time David opened the lounge door - his Granny was standing beside him. We found lying at the door a potato scoop from the kitchen. I switched out my light, joined my son and his Granny in the lounge. No sooner had we done this than a wooden coat-hanger came from I don't know where, struck our fire surround, bounced off and landed in the centre of the lounge floor. By 11p.m. the tapping had started. My brother and his wife and daughter arrived en route to their own home. The purpose of their visit was to make sure things were quiet; they had been told to do this every night. The boys were asked by their uncle Hugo Schwarz to go and lie on the top of their Granny's bed, and he would also lie beside them.'

It should be mentioned that at this stage of the case, Hugo Schwarz was still convinced that it was all trickery.

'They agreed to this; no sooner were they lying on the bed when the wall behind the bed head seemed to be hit by a sledgehammer. The noise of that one blow brought the boys and their uncle out of the room like bolt lightning.'

Once again they decided to move to the Schwarz's. The boys, Mr Uppingham's brother-in-law and he remained downstairs and the women retired upstairs to the bedroom. David was lying on a couch trying to sleep when the old familiar noise began again, only this time a cushion he was lying on began to rotate under his head as if someone was trying to pull it from under his head. Then the zip of his sleeping bag was seen to keep unzipping itself.

'This went on until 2.30 am when we all fell asleep exhausted.'

They stayed there at the Schwarz's for a number of nights. On one particular night all was peaceful for about 10 minutes after the women had retired upstairs then screams were heard from upstairs.

'On investigation it was found that a large double bed on which my wife and mother-in-law were lying was mysteriously pulled from the wall onto the centre of the floor and then pushed back with a bang against the wall. After doing my best to calm the women down I returned to the lounge where I had asked my brother-in-law to stay with the boys: apparently while I had been upstairs the camp beds which the boys were lying on had slid to and fro across the carpet, accompanied by scratching and rubbing and banging noises.'

Mr Uppingham's statement goes on listing phenomenon after phenomenon, indeed all sorts of malicious things had happened although the house had been locked up and there did not seem to be any sign of anyone breaking in.

By now the families were on the verge of a collective nervous breakdown. They were visited by a Mrs Reid, a professional medium. She discussed the whole problem with them and decided she had to rescue the three miners whose spirits were 'earth-bound'. She held a service and afterwards assured the Uppinghams that they had nothing more to fear because the three miners' spirits had now found rest.

While the Uppinghams were back home the Schwarz's in the meantime had been having a bad time, especially when Ian visited them. It was noticed that in his presence electrical gadgets kept blowing fuses. They never found out why this was so.

So ended the second phase.

At this time I had still not appeared on the scene but now I was contacted through a mutual friend and joined up with Max Magee to investigate because a third phase was starting about 3rd February 1975 which went on until 23rd May 1975. Now there were daytime happenings. There were noises of course; the sledgehammer sound was well in evidence, movements of articles occurred again and the family seemed more threatened. It was perfectly obvious that this was a family who were terrified. It was also noticeable that the Dutchman, who had formerly been convinced that it was trickery, was not now nearly so sure; he himself was in a highly nervous state since these inexplicable things began happening in his own house.

One of the incidents is thought-provoking. Mrs Schwarz told me she possessed a polystyrene blockhead on which she kept a dress wig. On going upstairs one afternoon she found the bed-clothes arranged as if there was someone in the bed and the polystyrene blockhead and the wig arranged on the pillow. 'I nearly died,' she said.

In this third phase a new element entered which caused Max and me a great deal of worry. Ian and David began to suffer what seemed to be involuntary limb movements of a very drastic sort, where they were practically tied up into knots and claimed that they were unable to control this. On one occasion I witnessed the younger boy David lying flat in his bed and it seemed for all the world as if he was on a trampoline being bounced horizontally off the bed to a height of 2 ft. I simply could not see how he could do this voluntarily. It was as if he was a rubber ball being bounced off the bed. Sometimes both boys experienced this, always ending with either or both of the boys being pushed off the bed, the bedroom subsequently becoming uninhabitable.

In addition to this they seemed to be governed by movements that ostensibly displayed the most intricate and skilled movements. On one occasion the Dutchman and one or two of the others were playing cards in the lounge, as they did very often to try and take the boys' minds off what was happening, when the movements began again.

Max Magee relates how on the second of May while they were in the midst of this strange phase of involuntary movements a remarkable episode occurred, witnessed by the family, and by the Dutchman. On this occasion the boys had been so disturbed by these involuntary movements that they were brought through from their bedroom and everyone congregated in the living-room. To occupy them, they were playing cards. Suddenly David started to throw his cards around as if compelled to do so. Ian began a sleight of hand routine which he had evidently never done before and has never done since. As the father, mother and brother-in-law described it, they said they would have been amazed if they had seen it onstage live or on TV because of the rapidity of the movement of the cards, the dexterity of the hand movements. Apparently he went through what they considered a brilliant sleight of hand performance and this unfortunately led them back to the feeling that there was a spirit in the place trying to possess them. About two months work by Max and I trying to wean them off this conviction that the house was haunted was apparently undone.

By this time the disturbances had become so severe that Max and I, in order to give the family what comfort we could, had taken to sleeping on alternate nights at the house. It was on one of these occasions that Max was able to tape the sledgehammer sounds and on another that I myself heard those sounds and saw the seemingly involuntary movements where the boys were knocked out of bed and almost tied in knots. The Dutchman told us that he had viewed a wardrobe which stood between the two boys' beds lean out from the wall and straighten up again, lean out again and fall. He was just in time to catch it. During the involuntary movements the boys seemed to mimic the noises by twisting round on the beds to hammer their feet on the walls. Needless to say they had not been seen to do this when the normal or abnormal noises had been heard by a large number of people. And in particular I noticed Ian twisting his legs round and actually having the strength to push the wardrobe completely away from the wall so that I had to catch it before it toppled over.

And so each night Max or I would spend the night at the Uppingham's house. Max relates how on one occasion when he was on call he was told things were very bad.

'I went to the house. There I found the Dutchman, a 16 stone, six foot-two man sitting astride the little 11 year old boy and being moved backwards and forwards as though being pushed by the little boy. Of course one can only work from visual evidence here and from the perspiration on his face and the desperation in his look it was difficult, to put it mildly, to believe that this was feigned on his part. It seemed a genuine case where a young boy was exerting such force that he was forcing this six-footer back again and again. I stood at the door listening to the noise and wondering if the inhibiting effect would work again here and then I got rather annoyed with the thing. When you have been sleepless for a number of nights for a few weeks you do begin to feel that this is just ridiculous so I walked in and said, "This is ridiculous. Stop it." And it stopped just like that. So I said "Good. Now we know we can inhibit this kind of movement."

Max also noted that the tape recording made at that time was not a very good one. The tape recorder worked perfectly well before and after, making good quality recordings but in addition to the sledgehammer sounds, there was a background noise level out of all proportion to anything heard before or since.(this background noise level also happened in the Fife case)

The sledgehammer effect is as if someone with an enormous sledgehammer was taking it and hammering it against the side of the house to such an extent that the whole house shook, a blow coming every 5 seconds or so, hour after hour, till in desperation one would say, 'Oh stop it.' And it would stop. For a while... On one occasion after a long interval of blessed silence Max said, 'I believe we will get to the bottom of this.' Immediately there was a sustained banging as if to say, 'Oh, no you wont!'

The third phase ended very suddenly. It ended by Max holding a service almost in desperation when the family were not present. I aided him. This was the 18th May. By this time we had formed a firm opinion that the boy Ian was at least the main focus though we also held the view that Mrs Uppingham showed signs of being a focus for the phenomena. We even wondered if Janet was a focus in the Schwarz's house.

Finally we decided to send Ian to his grandparents in the North of Scotland and the phenomena quietened down considerably. We cannot however be sure that this course of action produced the improvement. We have a statement that some phenomena did occur in the north of Scotland while Ian was there. Other phenomena occurred at a later date when Ian was taken by his uncle to Spain and we have a statement about that as well. From then until the following year everything became quiet so that we wondered if the three weeks Ian was up north, away from his family and school, which he disliked, away from the whole centre of his unhappiness, had had a marked beneficial effect.

There are many unanswered questions about this case, indeed about any poltergeist case. How does 'it' produce these movements, some crude, others tantalisingly skilled? Science remains baffled.

All we can do, as investigators, is to study these cases and compare notes.

There are many well documented cases of poltergeist activity which are well known to psychical researchers, but not really well known by the person in the street who has not investigated these matters before. I now give you a flavour of two such cases. If this peaks your appetite then you are may wish to obtain further literature to give you the full gamut of the phenomena, such as in the following case.

The Enfield Case

Many 'classic' cases of poltergeist activity display similar phenomena to those described by myself in this book. Indeed many are much more violent. Such a well-researched case and possibly one of the best known is the Enfield poltergeist.

The Enfield poltergeist made itself known on August 31st, 1977, and within a week it had made the front page of the *Daily Mirror*, the BBC lunchtime news and LBC's Night Line programme, and brought SPR member Maurice Grosse to the scene, followed a week later by author, Guy Lyon Playfair, both of whom stayed on the case until it ended in October 1978, apart from a few minor after-shocks a few months later.

By then, they had managed to observe examples of just about every kind of poltergeist phenomenon ever reported, from knocks on floors and walls, movement of furniture (witnessed on the very first day by a police constable), throwing of small objects, regular and inexplicable malfunction of cameras and tape recorders, outbreaks of spontaneous combustion, interference with bedclothes, and most intriguing of all, the apparent passage of matter through matter. Some of the incidents were alarming, such as the pulling of a built-in gas fire out of the wall, bending the quarter-inch pipe attached to it, and the flight across the room by its heavy iron grille which landed on a pillow within inches of the head of one of the children. On one occasion, Maurice and Guy witnessed ten incidents in a single minute, after which they stopped trying to keep count.

Events then became even more bizarre when twelve year-old Janet was seen levitating by the lollipop lady across the street. A tradesman passing the house saw a heavy cushion appear on the roof in his direct line of vision. Janet also described 'going through the wall' into the (locked) semi-detached house next door – hard to believe until a book of hers was later found there. Then she began to speak in the voice of an old man who announced that he had lived in the house, gone blind and died in the chair downstairs. The family knew nothing about the former tenant, but this was confirmed by the man's son several years later after he had heard Maurice Grosse describing the incident on a radio programme.

This is only the barest outline of a case that attracted worldwide media attention and has been featured in several radio and TV documentaries. There was more – much more: the transcript of Maurice and Guy's tape recordings runs to more than six hundred pages, and the whole story from start to finish is told in Guy's best-selling book *This House is Haunted*, now available in an updated edition from White Crow Books. I think you will agree that there has never been a case quite like it.

In 2011, Janet appeared on daytime TV with Guy Playfair and held firmly to her assertions that these events did happen and were absolutely true. Her very firm live comment to the young sceptical psychologist who was present, was "You wasn't there luv, you don't know."

The Cardiff Poltergeist

Another well researched classic case was lovingly nicknamed, Pete The Poltergeist.

Professor David Fontana of Cardiff University, who investigated the Cardiff poltergeist case over a two year period from June 1989 to early 1992, found that no living young people were involved and no adult mischief-makers. He was called in by the SPR who had been contacted by the proprietor John Matthews of the lawnmower repair workshop and the adjoining garden-accessories shop where the disturbances were taking place. In his investigation, David was fortunate enough to witness many of the phenomena himself. As an active researcher, David was well aware that although one can become intellectually convinced by the testimony of people of obvious probity, there is nothing like the emotional conviction generated when one experiences paranormal phenomena oneself.

When David arrived John Matthews told him that the poltergeist had first made his presence known on a quiet Saturday afternoon. John and one of his workmen were watching television in a shed when in succession the noises of large stones hitting the shed's roof startled them. At length, with no sign of the stone-throwing stopping, the police were called, in the hope that they would find and arrest the culprits. The police could find no one responsible. Further incidents began to happen inside the workshop. They included the throwing of coins, bolts and small stones against the walls of the workshop. There was also the arrival of objects of unknown origin such as a pen and keys, and old pennies dating from 1912 that seemed to fall from the ceiling or were found on the work surfaces. Tools on racks would be set swinging. David, in his account of the case, also includes as events

> '. . . blue flames emerging from a brass shell case which was kept as an ornament in the workshop and which was sometimes thrown violently around the room, planks of wood apparently too heavy to be thrown by hand hurled from the yard through the open door of the workshop, stones thrown at Pat, John's wife, while she was in the toilet at the back of the workshop with the door locked, dust thrown down John's collar and that of a business associate who worked with him, and loud knocks on the windows of the shop when no one was visible outside.'

In fact there were five principal witnesses involved, John, Pat, Paul (Pat's brother), Yvonne (Paul's wife), and Michael, John's business associate. All were respectable, middle-aged people and, as David got to know them, he gained a favourable impression of their honesty. They had all witnessed many of the events. John's daughter, a psychiatric nurse, was also convinced of the paranormal nature of the case, having herself witnessed some of the events. In addition there had been visitors to the establishment who had been startled by inexplicable incidents. In fact, one of the reasons John had called in the SPR was a worry that someone would be hurt by an object thrown by the poltergeist. He also had feared that potential customers would be frightened away if they saw objects moving mysteriously.

John told David that after a day of irritating incidents involving stone-throwing by 'Pete' the poltergeist, as they had named him, and still striving for a normal explanation, he persuaded Michael and an employee to join him after closing time in the retail shop. With their hands flat on the counter they still heard the stone-throwing sounds coming from the empty workshop. The employee suggested that they asked Pete to fetch named tools from the workshop into the retail shop. To their bemusement this was done, each tool arriving as if falling from the ceiling and materialising on the way down. The interval between request and response was so short that John told David that if the request had been made to him he could not have found the tool and delivered it in that short space of time.

The responsive nature of many of Pete's actions is one of the most fascinating features of the case. Apart from the seemingly random nature of many of the poltergeist's actions, there were times when onlookers could get Pete to play 'games' with them. It began when, during a period of stone-throwing, John picked up one of them and irritably tossed it back into the corner of the workshop from which many of the stones appeared to come. A stone was returned. John repeated his action several times with the same response. Pat herself was successful when she threw stones. When David next visited the workshop he tried it for himself several times. Each time a stone was returned, always from the same corner, which came to be known as the active corner. Stones thrown into the other corners elicited no response. They never saw the stones thrown back towards them while they were in flight. They would hear each stone strike the wall or one of the metal storage shelves with a characteristic 'ping' then clatter to the floor.

David was forced to the conclusion that fraud (for what possible motive!) was just not reasonable.

Another 'game' and one that Pete proved far better at than David and the others involved the brass 25-pounder shell case from the Second World War, kept in the workshop as a souvenir. John placed it at the far end of the workshop and tried to hit it with some of the small stones often found on the floor when the workshop was opened in the morning. He was unsuccessful. On an impulse he shouted 'All right, Pete, you hit it.' Immediately a stone pinged loudly on the shell case. On his next visit to the premises, David was told about this incident and tried the 'game' for himself. David told me that although he was unable to hit the shell case, Pete, when he asked him to hit it, did so. In fact, from a distance of 20 feet, neither David nor John was ever able to hit the shell case by throwing stones at it. Pete, seemingly, could do so at will.

The bizarre nature of the case, together with the necessity of accepting the existence of an intelligence behind the cooperation of the poltergeist, was heightened by the 'money' phenomenon. Three 1912 pennies had arrived in response to John and the other members of the family suggesting to Pete that he should try to bring them rather more useful things – like money. Now, intrigued by this logical answer to their request, John asked Pete for a rather more useful sum of money. Over the following weeks, crumpled £5 notes were found in the workshop and the retail shop when John opened up in the morning. They were either on the floor or pinned to the ceiling with the sharp needle of a carburettor float. David was told that the sum total received in this way exceeded £100. The question of where the money came from remained unanswered. It did not come from cash held in the shop.

Paul claimed that on three occasions he had seen the apparition of a young boy in the workshop. His first experience was when he entered through the outer door. The boy was sitting on the top shelf in the active corner. Paul described him as about twelve years of age, solid and detailed except for the face and hands. The face was simply an oval. The figure was seen sitting upright although a living boy would have had to crouch because of the lack of headroom. Paul said the ceiling immediately above the boy's head seemed to have dematerialised. The second time Paul saw the boy he was working with John on a petrol engine on the floor between them. Paul saw the boy behind John and called out to John to look up. The apparition disappeared. As it did so a large stone hit the petrol engine with great force. The third time Paul saw the boy; he was leaving the workshop, preparing to lock up. The figure appeared to be waving, as if to say farewell.

It can be a mistake by some investigators to jump at a seemingly plausible solution and neglect considering every other theory that has been proposed to account for poltergeist phenomena. David did not make that mistake. In his account of the Cardiff case he describes how he carefully addressed the likelihood of fraud, which he had to dismiss. He also assessed the likelihood of seismic activity and ground water, two theories previously put forward by rather sceptical psychical researchers but not subscribed to by many practical researchers of poltergeist cases. He had to dismiss them as not even marginally plausible, considering the responsive nature of Pete. The idea that the phenomena are produced by the unconscious psychokinetic activity of an unhappy living person, usually young, did not fit the fact that the five people were middle-aged and there was no evidence of any particular rage or emotional frustration in any of them. The dictum of Sherlock Holmes irresistibly comes to mind. When you have eliminated the impossible, then whatever remains, however improbable, is the truth. Life, and paranormal phenomena seeking a solution, is of course not quite as simple as Holmes made out but should be kept in mind by detectives and psychical researchers

The idea that the workshop was haunted by something connected to a young boy gained some support when John told David that there was a local rumour that a small boy had been killed in a traffic accident just outside the premises. When this rumour appeared in a national newspaper, David was approached by the young boy's elder brother, now grown-up, who confirmed the death. David cautiously states in his report that he had to consider it as a possible cause of the phenomena.

The old workshop and retail shop were subsequently transformed into a restaurant and David heard no further details of this case. However, to this day, from time to time, John and his wife appear to get an occasional visit from Pete as they can be sitting at home when a one pound coin drops into their tea, with a 'plop', and sometimes an orange appears from nowhere on the draining board of their kitchen. Seemingly it was known to them that Pete did not like oranges.

The Case of the Jealous Farmhouse

There is no doubt that much of the uncertainty and fear experienced by Mr and Mrs David Grant (pseudonyms) in their physically (and psychically) disturbed farmhouse stemmed from the total unpredictability and seemingly haphazard nature of the events thrust upon them. They were a professional level-headed couple, introduced to me through a mutual friend. They told me that they had leased the farmhouse in January and lived in it until November of the same year. The house is isolated but for two others in its vicinity and is situated in the Lake District a few miles from beautiful Lake Ullswater in wooded countryside. Sheila and David Grant had leased the farmhouse to live in while their new house was being built fairly nearby. I took Professor Roy to visit them where they told us about the strange incidents that occurred during the stay in the farmhouse. These incidents had reduced both of them to such a state of extreme nervousness that at the end of their stay they had left the farmhouse one night before they were due to move into their new home. There, they slept the first night on the floor of the new but unfurnished house rather than remain for one more night in the old farmhouse. They admitted, sheepishly, that in this way they had behaved irrationally and now marvelled that their experiences could have made them act in such a seemingly irrational manner.

The farmhouse was joined to a larger, unoccupied mansion house. Both buildings had stood there surrounded by fields and woods for centuries. The farmhouse was two-storied, the ground floor containing a lounge, on the side facing the road, together with a kitchen and dining room. The upper floor contained two bedrooms above the lounge, with a bathroom and veranda above the kitchen and dining room. Some distance away from the mansion and farmhouse within sight of them, stood a new house inhabited by Mr and Mrs Young, who leased the farmhouse to Mr and Mrs Grant. There was a small stream in a small gully in the vicinity of the house and when the Grants took the lease, they were told that in the dead of night people living in the farmhouse often heard it gurgling and bubbling over the pebbles and rocks in its bed. The Youngs hoped the Grants would not be disturbed by it.

David and Sheila Grant were happy at first with their lease. It gave them a comfortable place to stay not many miles from the site on which their new house was being built. But as time passed, various incidents in the farmhouse increasingly bothered them. Lately they had found the atmosphere in the house ominous and oppressive so that Mrs Grant in particular became nervous and apprehensive whenever she went upstairs to the bedrooms or the bathroom.

Sometime after they took possession of the house, Sheila Grant found herself wakening about two am to hear the sound of people "leaving as if after a party" from the mansion house adjoining the Grants' dwelling. The sounds, just on the border of earshot, gave her the impression of laughter, of farewells being said, of a mixture of footsteps and other noises associated with people departing. She remembered that the house next door was empty and woke her husband. Mr Grant could not hear the sounds although both the Grants heard the murmur and gurgle of the burn nearby. At first Mrs Grant wondered if she could have misinterpreted the noise of the stream as the sound of people. But the incident was repeated a number of times for a period of about one month. On each occasion Mrs Grant would be awakened about two am by noises. When she wakened her husband, he would hear nothing but the burn.

Other incidents were beginning to occur. During the day Mrs Grant wore a cross on a chain around her neck. Each night in preparing for bed she would take it off and place it on a stand on her dressing table. One morning when she went to pick it up she found that it was missing. Mr Grant denied having moved it and although Mrs Grant searched for the cross she was unable to find it. She had long reconciled herself to its loss when, months later, it turned up in her purse. She was flabbergasted. She said: "I couldn't believe it. The cross is so big that I could not have had it in my purse for any length of time without seeing it." Both David and Sheila Grant assured us that she is a person of routine never or hardly ever varying her habits. To this day the loss of the cross and its recovery remains inexplicable to the Grants.

But, by now, other articles were going missing. Every so often a shoe would be lost - not always the same shoe and sometimes a pair of shoes. The missing articles would turn up some time later, having been in limbo, as it were, for days or sometimes weeks. However, some of the items were never returned.

On another occasion Mr Grant found a packet of cigarettes missing from his jacket pocket. Rather more alarmingly he also found that he had lost his wallet containing money, credit cards and other personal items. He had been driving the car and had parked it outside before entering the house. When he discovered the loss of wallet and cigarette packet he returned to the car and searched it thoroughly, pursuing the rather unlikely probability that they had fallen out while he drove the car. His search produced nothing. He returned to the house. Recalling that he had just driven from the village where he had filled the car with petrol, he wondered if the missing items had fallen out in the village or if he'd left them in the petrol station. Sheila persuaded her husband to have some tea before returning to retrace his steps. After a cup of tea he went upstairs to the bathroom. On leaving the bathroom he saw, through the open bedroom door, one of the two beds it contained. The room was a spare bedroom never used. To David Grant's utter astonishment, he saw his lost wallet lying on the bed. Thoroughly bemused, he checked the contents and found that nothing was missing. To add to the mystery, a short time later his cigarettes were found in the glove compartment of his car. This may not seem to be unusual, but normally they would not have been placed there by Mr Grant who, from the driver's seat, could not easily use the glove compartment as he has a weak left hand. He swears that he never put them there.

During their stay in the farmhouse, the Grants lost other objects; among them Mrs Grant's spare spectacles.

They would sometimes arrive home at night to find lights on in the house. Both were certain they had left none on.

On one occasion in the early summer Mr Grant woke one night to see a shimmering luminous figure at the bottom of the bed. The torso was visible. The figure had long golden hair and stood with its hand or arm across its face. Strangely enough, David Grant felt no fear or panic during the experience. He got out of bed and the figure disappeared. Mr Grant returned to his bed and lay down. To his astonishment, he saw some time later a second golden figure. This one gave the impression of being bald: again its hand or arm was positioned across its face. When we asked Mr Grant what his reaction was, he said sheepishly "For some reason I decided to wave to it. Whereupon, it disappeared!" Mrs Grant slept throughout this episode. In the morning, Mr Grant told her of his nocturnal visitors.

Whereas it would appear that early on in their lease of the farmhouse it was Sheila Grant who experienced most incidents, a reversal took place later on in the lease, with David Grant being more often troubled.

On another occasion he found himself awake, seeing faces looking in at the bedroom window which, it will be recalled, was on the second storey of the farmhouse. This window was made up of many small panes. He said the faces were small, with one at each windowpane. They had a greyish blue tinge and were expressionless.

Around the month of July, he again found himself awake in the middle of the night. On a wall of the bedroom he saw a band of light, orange-red and undulating up and down. It also seemed to him that the window and the bench below it had disappeared. In the far corner of the room a dark, draped and cowled figure was outlined. The band of light and the figure were seen at the same time. Mr Grant felt panic. It should be noted that there were no street lights in the area and certainly no passing traffic.

In August the Grants bought a large double bed which they stored at first on its side in the spare bedroom. They then transferred it to the bedroom they used and slept in it, their heads towards the window. One night they both awoke to see five balls of light hovering near the bottom of the open bedroom door. For a time the white balls of light hovered there then moved slowly to the foot of the bed. When they reached the foot of the bed the Grants managed to break free of their stupefaction, dived towards the door and switched on the bedroom light. The balls of light disappeared.

From then on until the end of their lease David and Sheila Grant slept with the light on. Things still happened. David, sleeping with a leg outside the covers, found his legs thumped by something invisible. A few weeks after the September weekend, the Grants were in the kitchen. It was daytime. They both heard a thud behind them. They turned round and saw a dead blackbird on the floor. There was no hole in the ceiling through which it could have come or any other aperture in the kitchen. The windows were closed. On examination the blackbird was found to be dried up as if it had been dead for some time. Mr Grant took the corpse outside and put it in the dustbin.

By now the Grants were in a highly nervous and even confused state and became increasingly so during the rest of their stay. Although they both had been happy at first in the farmhouse, they began to form a strange impression as the atmosphere of the house seemed to grow more ominous and oppressive. They began to fear that the house did not want them to leave. In some totally irrational way they even felt it resented the fact that they were going to leave it for a new house. Talking it over - well outside the house! - they decided to leave the day before the last night they were due to sleep in the farmhouse in case - they told us somewhat sheepishly - something nasty happened to prevent them leaving. And so they departed to sleep that last night on the floor of the new, unfurnished house rather than remain for one more night in the old farmhouse.

Mr and Mrs Grant did tell the Youngs, from whom they had leased the farmhouse, about their experiences. Mrs Young admitted that at times when she was looking out of the window of her house, not too far away, she would sometimes see a light on in the old house though not always from the same room.

An electrician whom the Grants had in to their new home to do some electrical work asked them: "Did you ever see anything "funny" in the Youngs` house?" They asked what he meant and he said that on one occasion when working alone in the old mansion house he felt a sense of extreme coldness and found he could not or dare not turn round, so sure was he that there was something behind him. Thereafter he refused to work alone at the house. The electrician also said that an old guy living at that time in the main (that is, the mansion) house once asked him: "Didn`t you ever hear the sound of horses and carriages leaving early in the morning?"

We asked the Grants if they had ever had similar experiences before they took the lease of the farmhouse. They said they had never had any such experiences elsewhere before or since (and did not want any) except for one possible incident in their new house which, they hastened to add, could well be natural and a coincidence. In the new house, on their sitting room wall, they had hung a picture of the old farmhouse in which they had had such a disquieting time. It fell off the wall one night because the cord suspending it had broken.

What are we to make of this case? The total sceptic, who is in the position of not having met Mr and Mrs Grant, has the freedom to say that it is possible that they were trying to hoax us, or that one of the Grants was trying to hoax the other, or they both were laughably imaginative and allowed themselves to be worked up by unusual non-paranormal events into a state of suggestibility bordering on hysteria and even hallucination. The idea that there is anything paranormal in this case, the sceptic may say, is ridiculous. With respect to the first hypothesis, we have to ask what motive the Grants may have had in trying to hoax us. They had been reluctant to tell us of their experiences, they both held responsible positions; they seemed honest and had nothing to gain in telling us a pack of lies. Meeting them, we formed the distinct impression that they were describing what they believed they had experienced in the farmhouse. Again, if for some reason Sheila Grant was trying to hoax her husband, the sceptic has to explain how she caused him to lose his wallet and cigarettes and induced him to "see" the figures at night and the luminous balls. Did she have the desiccated blackbird hidden on her ready to throw surreptitiously behind her? Why, in the new house in which they have lived for quite a number of years now, did she not continue to trick her husband? It could not have been that she was trying to force him to quit the farmhouse and live in a brand-new house: there was no need for that for they were already waiting to do so.

Contrariwise, if it was a case of Mr Grant hoaxing his wife, for some reason, did he place a tape recorder in the empty house next door, timed to go off at two am to play the sound of "people leaving a party", which sound he would then deny hearing? Did he hide a number of his wife's shoes, or her spare spectacles, or her cross? Did he make up his alleged experiences? Did he obtain and produce the blackbird? But then, Mrs Grant stated that she also had seen the five luminous balls of light. And again, one might ask why it ceased when they moved into the new house?

Let us leave the unconvincing hoax theories and consider the "imagination" theory. Did Mrs Grant misinterpret the sound of the burn as the mingled noises of people saying farewell, footsteps, laughter? And do so for an entire month? Even after Mr Grant told her that although he could hear the burn he could not hear the people?

Certainly, missing objects are not the result of imagination. They went missing, sometimes for months. But did Mrs Grant, "a person of routine", inadvertently put the cross in her purse so that it lay there for months undiscovered even though it bulked large therein? The missing shoes do not seem to be the result of careless misplacing, nor does the incident of David Grant's wallet and cigarettes. He certainly did not remember placing the wallet on the bed in the spare room where he found it. It would almost appear that if such incidents were the result of lapses of memory or inattention, such lapses on both their parts would seem to have been of such pathological proportions as to play havoc with their everyday professional lives.

The luminous figures, the band of light, the change in the room structure, the five balls of light are difficult to interpret. David Grant saw them all; Sheila Grant saw the five balls of light. Hypnagogic phenomena (imagery seen when descending into sleep) and hypnopompic phenomena (imagery seen when awakening from sleep) hardly fit the bill here, especially when both David and Sheila saw the luminous balls. We find it difficult to dismiss these accounts as imagination or hypnagogic or hypnopompic phenomena.

Finally, the dead blackbird was real. It was a real corpse that Mr Grant put in the dustbin and two intelligent people could find no explanation for its appearance in the kitchen.

Taken by itself, the farmhouse case is intriguing and puzzling. Taken in conjunction with a host of other inexplicable cases encountered by ourselves and other psychical researchers it strengthens the age-old statement of Hamlet, "There are more things in heaven and earth, Horatio, than are dreamt of in your philosophy".

Built in with the Bricks

Archie Roy has sometimes remarked that ordinary houses seem far more popular with ghosts these days than stately homes and castles, as if comfort was a consideration in the psychic world. Certainly more of the cases he has been called out to have involved modern houses than other habitations.

The following is an account of an intriguing case given to me by him.

Some years ago, in a little West of Scotland town, the Rev. Max Magee and Archie had a case that perplexed them greatly for some time before the explanation, if explanation it was, presented itself to them. Max, Chaplain to Strathclyde University students was called in by the Clerk to the Presbytery who knew of his experience in psychic matters. In his turn the Clerk had been consulted by the local minister of religion to whom the family concerned had fled for help.

On the first visit to the town, Max and Archie interviewed Mr and Mrs Wood. Peter was a pleasant young man, perhaps thirty years of age, his wife Karen a year or two younger. They had one child, Katie, a little girl of three. Both parents confirmed as far as possible each other's story. Both parents seemed sensible young people, though extremely worried ones when we saw them.

They had been very pleased to get their new council house. They were the first tenants and they had had a lot of fun furnishing it and arranging things just as they wanted them. Katie had a little nursery along a short corridor from her parents' bedroom. Downstairs there was a very handsome lounge and a modern fitted kitchen.

The first phenomenon could be called 'the footsteps'. On a number of occasions the Woods, lying in bed at night, heard light quick footsteps coming along the corridor towards their room. When they first heard it, they thought Katie had somehow managed to get out of her cot and was coming to them. But the bedroom door did not open and Karen, getting up and going to the nursery, found the little girl fast asleep. This happened several times before Karen stopped checking. She said to us: 'We would lie listening to these footsteps and I would almost wish that something else would happen. In fact, one night when I was in the bath, I saw the door handle slowly move down and up. Peter denied that he was responsible and Katie was in her cot when it happened.'

On occasion, they said, visitors, sitting in the lounge downstairs, would hear the footsteps upstairs and make some remark like, 'There isn't another child upstairs, is there?'

One evening, when Peter was away on business, Karen had put Katie to bed and was downstairs watching television in the lounge. She fell asleep to waken some time later with a start. She knew it must be very late for the TV screen showed the blizzard-like effect sometimes seen when the programmes have ended but the TV hasn't been switched off. With a feeling of dread, she saw, over by the fireplace, the tall dark figure of a woman dressed in black.

'And hating me,' said Karen. 'She didn't speak but she was resenting me. And I knew she wasn't real.'

'What did you do?' I asked.

'I don't know how I did it but I darted upstairs, got into bed and put my head under the bed clothes.'

The next time Peter went away on business, Karen invited an old friend, a nursing sister from the Royal Infirmary, to stay the night. In the morning they found that each of them believed the other had got up in the middle of the night; half-aroused from sleep, they had seen a figure 'in a flowing negligee sort of gown' coming back to bed. Each denied getting up.

The final incident that drove the family from the house occurred when both parents were in bed. Shrieking with terror, their daughter rushed into their room, climbed onto the bed and burrowed in between them. It was a long time before they calmed her down and got a coherent story out of her.

She had found herself downstairs in the lounge where a 'monster' had attacked her and tried to choke her. She had managed to break free and flee upstairs. Both parents tried to convince her that she had simply had a nasty dream. Both parents maintained however that their daughter was not given to nightmares. In any event the child's terror, together with the other incidents, communicated itself to them and they felt unable to stay in the house.

There are quite a few reasons other than the paranormal why a house is alleged to be haunted. The tenants may want to be re-housed to a better habitation or a more salubrious neighbourhood and, in the absence of any of the more ordinary ways of persuading the authorities to carry out their wishes, pretend that their house is haunted. Or there may be physical, natural phenomena, unrecognised as such, that lead the family to a genuine belief that they are the target of mischievous or malevolent spirits, House creaks and trains of raps can occur when there is a change in temperature, especially if the house is old. Sounds travel and can result in whispers being heard that actually originate in an adjoining dwelling. A water hammer - an airlock in the plumbing - can alarm the family by a sudden peremptory loud series of booming sounds, to be transformed into a poltergeist by the family which has just been watching "The Amityville Horror" or "The Exorcist" on TV.

And, of course, there are those unfortunates, mentally disturbed people whose delusions take the form of believing that aliens are beaming death-rays at them, or that the Devil is living in their cellar, waiting to get them, or that they are haunted.

In the case of the Woods, none of the usual normal reasons seemed to apply. Max and Archie therefore decided to pay a visit to the house, this time accompanied by Mr Albert Best the well-known Glasgow medium whom we both knew to have a genuine psychic gift. Without telling him where we were going, or anything about the case other than that a young couple seemed to need our help, we drove to the Woods' house. Peter Wood was present when we entered the house.

In such cases Albert Best finds it useful to wander about the house, waiting for impressions to come to him. He interprets these impressions in a frankly spiritualistic way. Ascending the inside stairs of the house, Albert walked slowly along the short corridor then stopped. He seemed to listen for a while before speaking.

> 'Children. There are children here. They come from the other side. They like to come here. It's a good loving atmosphere here so they like to come and play here.'

We went downstairs. In the lounge he halted, looking fixedly towards the massive fireplace, a handsome feature of the room built of genuine stones, and rubbed his hands together as if cold.

> 'Oh, it's different here. There's a woman over there. By the fire-place. An old woman. She sees us. And she doesn't like us. She's confused. She's saying "What are all these people doing in my house"'

Peter Wood watched and listened in obvious bewilderment and scepticism. 'But no-one has stayed in this house apart from us. We're the first family here.'

Albert nodded. He walked across to the fireplace and paused. 'I'll try to get some more information.'

Albert Best as a medium is noted for the accuracy of names and addresses he obtains, unlike many other mediums, who, although they may have a genuine psychic gift, often find it difficult to get names and addresses. It is possible that Albert is good at this because for many years he was a postman in Northern Ireland and may have become conditioned into associating names with addresses.

'I get the name Baird Street.'

Peter Wood said, 'That's where we got the stones.'

It turned out that Peter and his father-in-law had built the handsome fireplace in the lounge, bringing the stones it was built of from a demolished cottage in Baird Street, on the outskirts of the town. The big stone over the fire itself had been the lintel of a window in the cottage. Albert turned his attention elsewhere again. After a while he said,

> 'I've finally managed to get through to her. She didn't know she's dead. She was ill for a long time before she passed over and in her confused state still thought she was in her own cottage. She couldn't understand why she was seeing strangers in her house. She's very sorry for the trouble she's caused and apologises. I've shown her how she can move on and she says there'll be no further trouble.'

Spiritualism of course teaches that we survive death and that some of us can get 'stuck' on the other side for one reason or another. We have come across a number of cases where such a hypothesis has to be taken seriously. Dr. Carl Wickland M.D., the American psychiatrist and author of *Thirty Years Among the Dead* subscribed to this theory. So does Edwin Butler; on the other hand there is also the psychometrist theory. It is the case that there are certain gifted people, psychometrists, given an object belonging to someone else, who can achieve some kind of strange rapport with that person be he or she living or dead. The psychometrist is then able to reel off all kinds of facts regarding that person's past, present and immediate future. The rapport can be so strong that the psychometrist not only seems to have that person present but can take on, or be 'overshadowed' by, the physical and mental characteristics and idiosyncrasies of that person. The stones that Peter and his father-in-law had used to build the fireplace had come from the ruined cottage. Did they act as 'objects' in the psychometrist theory, enabling Albert to enter into rapport with a former owner of the cottage? Or is it true that some of us become, on the other side of death, 'Earthbound', in the spiritualist term, destined to hang around in a confused, dreamlike state, bewildered by a mixture of data perceived from two levels of being, impinging at times in a troublesome way on this facet of reality?

It would be nice to be able to say that Albert's intervention solved the problem. It would have tied the case up neatly. Certainly the family were encouraged by this 'explanation' to return to the house and certainly the old lady was never seen again, which was consistent with the hypothesis that her Earthbound shade or spirit or whatever had been built in with the bricks, so to speak, and subsequently released by Albert.

On the other hand, some phenomena were reported to us thereafter by Mr and Mrs. Woods. On one occasion they returned to the house one evening and found that all the drawers in their bedroom had been removed from the dressing table and wardrobe and laid neatly on the floor. Nothing was missing. On other occasions a dog was seen and reported running upstairs in the house by a number of different people catching glimpses of the animal. No dog was found upstairs. Another of the strange happenings of the time involved a conviction of Karen Woods as she lay in bed that on some nights there was a presence in the bed with her and Peter that gripped her ankles. In spite of such phenomena, real or fancied, however, the Woods' family remained in their house and quite soon, as often happens, no further phenomena were reported.

At times since, however, Archie and I had wondered what might have happened if Peter and his father-in-law had decided not to build a fireplace in the house but used the old cottage's stones to build a rockery in the garden. Would the house have escaped 'haunting' but would sensitive enough people have experienced rather unnerving phenomena in the vicinity of the rockery? We shall never know.

And now a case with 'less discarnate' influence - a cautionary tale.

Just a few years ago I was called to a household in Fife in Scotland where disturbances, which sounded similar to reported phenomena in "poltergeist" cases, had been reported.

I drove Archie Roy to the location and after a fairly lengthy journey we met a very friendly, well-educated but worried family who were at their wits end in trying to deal with some very strange occurrences.

The mother, let us call her Ann, and daughter, Jill, lived together in the family home from Monday to Friday but every weekend the daughter was sent to live with her 80 year-old grandmother, a mile or so away. The reason for this was that Ann had a new male companion, who stayed with her at the weekend in the family home while Jill was sent off to the grandmother's house for that period of time. After a few weeks passed, strange things began to occur in the grandmother's home. As there was only one double bed in this house the females shared the bed each weekend.

With the two of them in it sometimes the bed would vibrate so violently at times that each bottom leg of the bed, not the headboard end, would lift off the floor in turn making a tick-tick tapping noise on the wooden floor. Then noises were subsequently heard occurring as if coming from the headboard of the bed, a sort of banging and cracking noise that I would best describe as a thwack, with some of the sounds being very loud indeed. The bed sometimes vibrated and shook so much that items would also fall off the bedside tables and smash onto the floor. When these events started to occur they would telephone for the mother, Ann, to come to the house and when she did things would calm down a bit and activity often ceased altogether.

One night on a particular weekend, the grandmother had asked another three male members of the family to inhabit the lounge while she and Jill tried to get some sleep. That evening the bed shook so violently that it nearly took off with both inhabitants screaming and yelling while the three male visitors tried, to no avail, to hold the bed end down; it was as though their combined pressure had no effect on it at all. They would all testify to this. Eventually everyone went through to the lounge and tried to catch up with some sleep for the rest of the night, wherever and whenever they could. As far as I am aware those three men never came back again.

Fearing that no one else would believe them, next evening Ann and Jill had the presence of mind to put a tape recorder under the bed to try to record the events. In fact this worked very well and it did record the tapping noises from the bed legs hitting on the floor and the cracks, thwacks and sometimes very loud bangs from the headboard. It is all in all quite impressive and not something which could be easily falsified.

I still have that tape recording in my possession to this day, and if the situation was not so stressful, it is amusing in as much as the grandmother did not seem to understand the concept of the tape recorder as she continually swore at the headboard during the more violent thwacks. This engendered some hysterical irrepressible laughter in Jill in an otherwise stressful situation, as she tried to stop her grandmother swearing by reminding her there was a tape recorder running. The response to this was 'What f....n tape recorder?

I would love to colour this chapter with some more of grandmother's expressions, but let us just say that she was not amused. Unless you have heard the actual sound of a "poltergeist" type of thwack, it is impossible to describe as it has a quality all of its own. It is as though the sound is being produced from inside the headboard and coming outwards. It would have been very difficult for an eighty year old and a thirteen year old to have stage-managed the sounds in these circumstances.

As the grandmother was now becoming quite distressed, for a few weekends after that Jill went to stay with an aunt. We have the aunt's testimony along with that of a person in her home to the fact that strange events also occurred in her home. A certain amount of cracks and bangs came from the skirting boards of this house, but they were not nearly as loud as those from the headboard in the grandmother's house, or nearly as frightening. Cups were smashed in the kitchen when no one else was in the room; a feeling of presence was often experienced throughout this very lovely home, and once, when Jill entered the lounge, all of the papers and items on top of the coffee table were whisked on to the floor, in full view of the other two people entering with her. This was something that did not normally happen when someone came into that room.

Meantime, during the week when Jill was in her own home, nearly every time she entered through the door of her bedroom there was a loud BANG like thunder which resonated throughout the room, leaving the people who witnessed the experience feeling rather shaken up.

Jill and her mother were becoming more and more worried as the days passed, fearing that something awful was upon them, or about to descend on them.

At this point they decided to call upon the services of the Christian Church. They tried various denominations, but the only person who would come to their home was a minister of the Church of England. They explained the situation and he said that he would say prayers in the bedroom and that things should then be all right. The mother asked him "But what if it is not alright?"—the reply was that he would then need to get permission from his Bishop to perform another ceremony.

The minister indeed said prayers in that room and made to take his leave. Ann stopped him and said "Before you go let Jill go into the room and see if it is ok". He agreed. As Jill walked into the room there was the same type of tremendous BANG, like a very loud clap of thunder, and the room seemed to vibrate. The minister was last seen running down the garden path with Ann yelling after him "What do we do now?" and his response, while continuing his run, was "I'll need to see the Bishop".

He never returned.

It was at this point that we were called in.

Jill was 13 years of age and had a lot of pent up emotional energy combined with the fact that she had also just reached puberty. It became very clear very quickly that she appeared to be the focus of all the strange happenings.

After hearing about the events here described and after a long investigation, as she had been quite athletic in the past, I advised Jill that perhaps she should restart circuit training, as she had not kept this up for some time; It was hoped that getting rid of some of her energy through this method might help in some way to diffuse her pent up emotion and hopefully the situation.

I also gave mother and daughter 15 minutes of time together every evening by suggesting that they sit together quietly at a set time and jointly follow a simple de-stressing technique which was designed just for them.

This appeared to work well.

It was suggested to the family that the phenomena should gradually lessen day by day and eventually cease completely over a period of two weeks or so.

Without going deeply into the actual investigation and having to reveal the family's personal details, two weeks later all was quiet and the phenomena had gradually waned over this period as we had suggested to them. Peace appeared to be restored.

About another week later I received a letter from the mother Ann, thanking me profusely for all of the help. To this day I have heard no more about it, which usually means that all is quiet.

However, psychical researchers know from experience, that if a stressful situation ever arises again in this family again, there may be a possibility of more phenomena occurring.

It should be noted that although the phenomena in this case were genuine, no mediums or sensitives were required in this case investigation.

Another interesting point for you to ponder is the fact that even when Jill left the aunt's house, small strength phenomena still occurred in it from time to time throughout the subsequent two to three weeks, although at a very low level this time and not in a frightening in manner in any way.

Some poltergeist-type activity always seems to require a level of stress in a household before activity begins. This family group did fit this requirement. In this case when the stress levels were lowered the phenomena gradually receded and eventually disappeared altogether. I do not pretend to have any explanations for the events; again I can only report the facts as they happened.

The phenomena involved in this type of case are fascinating, as are the resolutions. It would appear that no-one fully understands the power of the human psyche but we can only poorly estimate the latent abilities we may possess, which under certain circumstances seem to externalise themselves in some kind of physical phenomena. People sometimes ask me why everyone under stress does not manifest poltergeist phenomena. My answer is 'I don't know.' Some people have nervous breakdowns, other do not.

It would therefore appear that incarnate, and discarnate, personalities can produce similar 'poltergeist-type' events. This should give us pause for thought in each case as a discarnate survival hypothesis is not always required, but sometimes it is the most parsimonious and 'best' explanation.

Chapter 5

DROP-IN COMMUNICATORS

T he term Drop-in communicator describes a situation, usually in a spiritual-type circle, or meeting, where a new communicator comes through unexpectedly and sometimes this person is unknown to any members of the circle or the medium and whose identity can be subsequently checked.

Robert Hartrick

Mediums are sometimes scoffed at by people who say that life after death cannot be a reality or even a possibility as no one ever came back through a medium from the so called dead to impart information that is of any real use, and that any information given is nothing other than the medium's wishful thinking or good guesswork. Perhaps the next account may change your opinion.

A few years ago a new manager of a large establishment was given the job of rescuing this said establishment from the financial downward spiral in which it found itself. His name was Robert Hartrick and he was a relatively young person who was fired up with enthusiasm. The idea was no doubt that a new broom would sweep away old ideas and methods to create a new beginning which would hopefully create conditions in which the establishment could flourish and turn the financial situation around. After a short time things were indeed altering and the finances of the establishment were on an upward turn and heading in an upwards spiral as things were picking up. It was therefore a great shock to everyone when this young man was tragically involved in a car accident and died of his injuries. Needless to say this all happened unexpectedly. Apart from the shock and sadness suffered after this tragic event, other people had then to build up a picture of the establishment's standing and, among other things, its financial position.

Following this event at least two strange things happened. I have a signed statement from Mr Lionel Owen, the president of the International Spiritualist Federation recounting the following:

"On the weekend of the 5th and 6th February 1994, a well-known Enfield medium was staying at my home because she was conducting a Saturday seminar and the two Sunday services at Longton Spiritualist Church. On the Saturday the medium, my wife Laura and I decided to hold a circle to communicate with spirit, something we often do when she visits our home. This normally took the form of spending about thirty minutes sitting for each person. On this occasion Laura was the person we sat for first and then it was my turn. I entered the trance state and two or three of my helpers spoke to the circle. Then it was the medium's turn and her helper spoke to us. As she was returning from her altered state of consciousness she began giving clairvoyance. She said Robert was contacting her, and because my own Uncle Robert works with me, especially during inspirational speaking, we assumed it was him. Very quickly she said 'No, it's Robert Hartrick and he is trying to tell me something about important papers which cannot be located.'"

The sitters in this circle knew nothing about missing papers, and this did not mean anything to them.

Around the same time as the above account, a gentleman who was affiliated to the establishment in question, had a dream about Robert Hartrick during which he had the impression that he was trying to tell him something by the way of passing information to him, but it was no stronger than that. He assumed that he had been dreaming and did not even mention it to anyone. The next evening he "dreamt" about him again, but this time he could see him holding up what looked like a brief case in his left hand and he was pointing to it repeatedly with his right hand. Once again he thought "what a strange dream" but did not give it any credence. This happened in an identical fashion the next evening but this time the man was also shown an image of a wrecked car, and a kind of zoom shot looking deep down under the dashboard and an impression of insistence to look in that place. Feeling a bit foolish, as this man was not a medium, he mentioned the events to a friend who suggested that he should find out where the wreckage of the car was being housed and go down to view it, just in case anything was lying in the wreck. He did so.

Nothing was to be seen at first; they looked in the door compartments, glove compartment, in the boot, under seats, in fact everywhere, and yet nothing was to be found. Now he did feel a bit foolish and thought that that was the end of it, but they sought assistance from the men in the wreckers yard and asked them to force some of the crushed metal apart under the dashboard and there it was - a slim-line briefcase with zippers on three sides - lying flat on a shelf styled piece of metal. I can just imagine their faces. When they opened the briefcase it contained a cheque for over two thousand pounds payable to the establishment along with other very important documents. After that the "dreams" stopped and the man never " saw" him again.

In case you have a suspicious mind, I can tell you that because the car in question was involved in a fatal road accident the police had to be notified of the intention to examine the car. They gave permission and were in attendance when the car was examined. Therefore the police themselves were witnesses to the recovery of the papers and money.

So in this case, it would appear this was one of the things that Robert could do after death as he wished to help the association that he had been working with. Here again we appear to have motivation and intention.

This seeming insistence demonstrated by a deceased person in trying to get a point across to someone living is a familiar aspect of the paranormal to psychical investigators. Upon investigating many avenues of reported paranormal phenomena there often seems to be this element of unfinished business, a task not finished, an expectation not fulfilled.

This sounds as though the men in white coats should be coming for psychical researchers such as ourselves, but if you take the time to study these things as pragmatically as possible and follow the evidence to a logical conclusion then you would have to look more favourably on the idea that not all happenings can be explained away under our normal frames of reference or scientific paradigms as we understand them at the present time.

It is almost as though Robert Hartrick "dropped in" to Lionel Owen's circle and also into the other gentleman's mind while he was dreaming.

In case you are confused with the term "drop-in communicator", I will expand on that term. If a person decided to go for a sitting with a medium he/she would be hoping to be given information from, for example, their grandmother, their father or someone else they hold dear. If someone else butted into the flow of information to say that they were Jean Williamson from a certain street in Leeds and gave all sorts of information that neither the sitter or the medium had knowledge of, or in truth were really interested in, that person who butted in would be called a drop in communicator, almost like an uninvited guest, but in this case you can't hide behind the door and pretend that you are not in. Similarly in some "circles" hoping to communicate with those who have passed on, a person may drop in who is totally unknown to any of the sitters. These drop in communicators can very often provide the best source of proof that information, previously unknown to any person present, can be transferred out with the normally accepted parameters of our understanding,

The previous account of the car crash victim giving information that subsequently proved to be correct reminds me of the saying "The proof of the pudding is in the eating." Would the unreasonable sceptic say that it was only by chance that a cheque for two thousand pounds and relevant documents were in a briefcase which no one else knew anything about, far less that they were in that particular location?

The sad answer is probably yes.

Multiple drop-ins

The Crash of the R101

One of the most respected and extensively studied mediums of the past was the late Mrs Eileen Garrett who not only cooperated on many occasions with psychical researchers and parapsychologists in their investigations but for many years supported the subject financially.

Perhaps the most fascinating and best known case involving her participation was concerned with the aftermath of the crash of the airship R 101 in France on the early morning of October 5th, 1930.

In considering that participation I must enlarge on the political and technological background leading to the disaster.

Major Oliver G. Villiers, a government minister from the home office, visited the well-respected trance medium Eileen Garrett. The information that he did receive in his sittings was certainly not that which he expected. This was around the time of the disaster of the crash of the airship R101. During his sittings with this medium it became crystal clear to him that statements were being made to him which purported to come from people who had been aboard the airship R101 when it crashed.

Through the trance mediumship of Eileen Garrett, Major Villiers had hours and hours of conversations with the aforementioned ostensible crew of the R101, who had been killed in the crash. For many reasons he became convinced that the people were indeed who they purported to be. Among these reasons was the fact that the detailed descriptions which each of the personalities gave were compatible with the knowledge and expertise of each of the deceased. For example, the structural engineer could give intricate details of flawed structures in the airship; details which any lay person, or indeed any person other than someone connected with that airship, could not possibly know. This was the case with each job title.

Such was the nature of the information given that Major Villiers had to do a great deal of seeking and searching in order that he might establish that the details given were correct. In every case the facts were exactly correct, as given by the "communicators" through the medium. The crew claimed that their motivation for speaking through Mrs Garrett was to set the records straight and also warn people of the mistakes and shortcomings that had led to the disaster.

This is again an account in which the information given could be verified; information that neither he nor the medium had, or could have had, any knowledge.

It was in the 1920's that the British Government authorised the building of two massive airships, the R100 and the R101. One man who certainly welcomed the new direction was Lord Thomson, the Secretary of State for Air. There was a round trip he wanted to make late in 1930 to an Empire conference in India and he thought that the R101 would be the right way to travel. In the event the team that built the R100 made better progress than the one working on the R101. Before the latter was completed, its sister ship on July 29 left England for Canada. It was a triumphant round trip, the airship returning some two weeks later. Encouraged by this, Lord Thomson put intense pressure on the R101 builders to hurry up and complete their job, dismissing or paying no attention to their warnings that various problems encountered necessitated delay and extended flight testing. In fact the two airships had independent teams of designers and builders, and it had become apparent to the R101 team at Cardington at least a year before that their dirigible had serious flaws in it. The diesel engines were too heavy for the power they provided, the outer canvas fabric was too flimsy - it had had to be replaced when it tore - the internal hydrogen-filled gasbags leaked, and an experimental fuel was unreliable. Several times in the flight-testing stages, the huge airship just managed to limp back to its base. The useful lift was found to be so minimal that in a last desperate attempt late in the day to snatch victory from the jaws of defeat it was sawn in half and a new mid-section inserted. It was now over 770 feet long. Press reports, however, were in general optimistic. On October 15, 1929, The Times aeronautical correspondent gave a glowing account of the airship's first flight the previous day lasting five hours which took it over London.

Lord Thomson continued his relentless pressure, even challenging the courage of people who would fly the huge ship, some of whom had been decorated fighter pilots in the recent war. On October 4th, at half past seven in the evening, the R101 left its mooring mast and set off for India. On October 5th, at five minutes past two in the morning, the airship crashed in flames near Beauvais in France. Six people survived, forty-eight died, among them Lord Thomson.

The main events however that make the tragedy of the R101 so important for psychical research are various sittings with the medium Eileen Garrett after the crash.

On the afternoon of October 7th, three days after the 101 disaster, the well-known psychical researcher Harry Price attended a sitting in his laboratory in London, where Price, Ian Coster, an Australian journalist and editor, Ethel Beenham, Price's secretary and Eileen Garrett met. Three months had passed since the death of Sir Arthur Conan Doyle, a staunch believer in post-mortem survival who had lectured world-wide in a long-sustained effort to persuade people that death was not the end. The meeting had been scheduled to give Doyle the chance to communicate if he had survived bodily death. In fact the meeting had a totally unexpected outcome. After Eileen Garrett had entered her trance and her control Uvani had surfaced and greeted the sitters, a communicator claiming to be a recently deceased psychical researcher, Baron von Schrenck-Notzing, came through briefly. He gave nothing of interest. Then without warning Mrs Garrett became extremely agitated, tears streaming from her eyes. The communicator and even Uvani were displaced in a storm of emotional distress and a strange voice, speaking swiftly, jerkily and in obvious anguish, began to deliver a stream of technical information about the myriad faults in the R101 that caused its destruction. Harry Price's secretary was hard put to take it all down in shorthand.

Before he was displaced Uvani managed to get the name Irving or Irwin. The captain of the R101 had of course been H. Carmichael Irwin. Now it appeared that the voice was desperately giving an account of the last flight-path followed and the ship's behaviour before it hit the ground and exploded. "We almost scraped the roofs at Achy. Kept to railway." Many more technical details were given. A major feature was the obsessive effort made by the communicator to get through in detail the disastrous nature of the airship's construction. Finally, after some 45 minutes of details, Uvani's voice returned. Sometime later a new communicator claiming to be Conan Doyle briefly surfaced. To the astounded and shocked sitters he was little more than an anti-climax.

At the time of the sitting little or nothing beyond the fact of the tragedy was known. To Price it was inconceivable that Mrs Garrett could have known the multitude of technicalities the anguished communicator blurted out or known definite reasons for the crash. Later he found that the statement that the doomed airship almost scraped the roofs at Achy, a very small village not marked on any but large-scale maps, must have been correct.

What Price was not aware of was that Major Oliver G. Villiers, of Air Ministry Intelligence, who knew almost everyone involved in the design, building and flight-testing of the R-101, had the already mentioned an experience of his own. Late in the evening of Saturday 25th October, sitting quietly by the fire, he was convinced he heard Captain Irwin's voice;

> "For God's sake let me talk to you. It's all so ghastly. I must speak to you. I must." A little later he heard the voice again. "We're all bloody murderers. For God's sake help me to speak with you."

Villiers consulted a friend who arranged a sitting with Eileen Garrett. Villiers met her anonymously on the evening of October 31st. It was the first of a series of seven remarkable sittings with the medium. At that sitting, Irwin came through and had a long and convincing technical discussion with Villiers. Villiers found himself listening to and questioning a communicator whose voice and mannerisms were Irwin's. Villiers got the irresistible impression that he was talking with someone - Irwin - who was giving an eye-witness account of the accumulation of faults and the moment-by-moment progression of the resultant disaster. After nearly an hour of this session, Irwin's voice said,

"No more now. You must come soon, as Scottie and Johnston say they must each come and give you their own story. It helps them. . . Come soon."

At the second sitting on November 2nd, Sir Sefton Brancker and Major G. H. Scott came through in succession. The former was the Director of Civil Aviation, British Air Ministry; the latter was the Designer of Airship Development. Both had died in the crash of the R101. After a technical discussion with Scott, who said that Colmore (Wing Commander Colmore who also died in the crash) wanted to speak to him, Villiers began to get an account of how, after the gang plank had been pulled back into the airship before take-off, some of them, including Scott, Irwin and Squadron Leader Johnston had told Lord Thomson that they were convinced that the flight had to be postponed. Thomson would have none of it.

The extraordinary series of sittings with Eileen Garrett continued until November 28th. At the third sitting Colmore came through, at the fourth Brancker, Scott and Colmore. There was some talk of missing documents at Cardington. At the seventh sitting Lieutenant Commander Atherstone came through and confirmed that he had kept two diaries, examination of which would be revealing because of the frank entries regarding the airworthiness of the airship.

Villiers contacted Sir John Simon and had lunch with him at the Royal Courts of Law. Sir John sent his assessor and registrar, L.F.C.Darby down to Cardington to look for those books and diaries that would give further information about the inadequate preparation for the journey of the airship. Nothing was found.

But that was not the end of the story. An account of Harry Price's sitting with Eileen Garrett appeared in Nash's Magazine on December 15th, 1930. The main emphasis was on Doyle but the R101 and the

Irwin communicator were mentioned. Price received a letter from Will Charlton, the former supply officer to the R101. He asked Price for a full transcript of the Garrett sitting. Price complied and Charlton showed Miss Beenham's account to a number of the technical staff at Cardington, asking them to assess the technicalities used by the Irwin communicators. The staff members were of the opinion that they made complete and dreadful sense.

In 1948, William H. Wood, a militant free-thinker and 'avid' atheist who had been a flight-lieutenant and squadron-leader in the First World War and who had known Irwin, found the Price-Coster story. He tracked down Charlton and Coster. As a consequence of his investigations, he eventually stated publically that he was convinced that Irwin had survived death. This put the cat among the pigeons in the atheistic world. However he remained a stern and unrelenting atheist - who now believed that we live after death. A unique position, I would think, in atheism.

In 1966, Sir Victor Goddard initiated a new investigation using a joint effort by the Royal Aeronautical Society and the Society for Psychical Research. A year later Michael Cox, a British film producer of documentaries, found and interviewed the widow of Lieut. Commander Atherstone. She showed him all her husband's papers, including the aforementioned 'missing' second diary. In it he found the following entry, dated a full year before the crash:

'There is a mad rush and panic to complete the ship.....It is grossly unfair to expect the officers to take out a novel vessel of this size.....the airship has no lift worth talking about, and is obviously tail heavy.'

Eileen Garrett died in 1970. Her own conclusion concerning mediumship stated: 'There is a positive and practical need for these communications to be studied'

The present author, along with Professor Archie Roy has spent the past 29 years, jointly, in just such a pursuit as suggested by Eileen Garrett. We have conducted many investigations and controlled experiments over this time, sometimes in conditions up to triple blind as far the mediums are concerned. The mediums gave of their time willingly as they were, and still are, of the same mind as Garrett - to try to discover the validity and methods of communication. Whatever else mediumship is, it is a transfer of information from one person, or source, to another person. Before pursuing the next account, it is worthwhile noting the thoughts of the first President of the Society for Psychical Research, Professor Henry Sidgwick when he said:-.

The records of experiments must depend ultimately on the probity and intelligence of the persons recording them, and it is impossible for us, as investigators, to demonstrate to persons who do not know us that we are not idiotically careless or consciously mendacious. We can only hope that within the limited circle in which we are known, either alternative will be regarded as highly improbable.

Runki

Let us now turn to the Icelandic 'drop-in' communicator Runki, who 'appeared' in the autumn of 1937, at sittings held in the Kvaran house. The medium on these occasions was Hafsteinn Bjornsson. He continued to appear a year later at sittings held in the Kristjansdottir house. In both locations he refused to give his name but stated repeatedly that he wanted his leg 'found'. When some months later Ludvik Gudmundsson joined the group Runki finally gave his name and the account of how he had drowned, we find him saying through the medium ' I walked over the kambinn [pebble beach] and reached the rock known as Flankastadaklettur which has almost disappeared now.' He drowned in October, 1879. The séance was held in the autumn of 1937. This is a slight but possibly interesting anomaly suggesting that the communicator was aware of a major change that had taken place in the rock since his death. His 'leg' was eventually found built into a wall, between two layers, in Gudmundsson's house and after the religious ceremony involving the burial of his thighbone, there was a reception at the presiding clergyman's home. Later, Runki said in a séance that he had been present on both occasions and how pleased he was at the events and even gave the names of the cakes served at the reception. The medium attended neither occasion.

Other 'drop-ins', communicating through the Icelandic medium Hafsteinn Bjornsson, were also studied by Professors Ian Stevenson and Erlendur Haraldsson. Runki Runolfsson, already described, made his presence known 58 years after his death. Like many other 'drop-ins' he had a purpose in doing so. He wanted one of his 'leg found' and re-united with the rest of his body (actually it was a part of his leg). This account raises a number of questions concerning the nature of any survival of death, the ability to communicate even after 58 years, and Runki's surprising and continuing interest in the state of his body even after the long period since his death.

Dr Alan Gauld has summed up what may be called the ideal 'drop-in' case which, he claims, 'pushes the super-ESP hypothesis to the verge of unintelligibility; indeed beyond that verge.'

Such a case would have the following features:

(a) The 'drop-in' communicator in question would have a strong and comprehensible reason for wishing to communicate; a reason clearly stronger than any which the medium might have for wishing to contact him.

(b) The information which he communicates would be such that the medium could not have obtained it all by extrasensory contact with a single living person, obituary notice, etc. (c) We can be tolerably certain that the medium could not have obtained the information by ordinary means.

After comparing the advantages of the survivalist theory over the difficulties and implausibilities of the super-ESP theory in such cases, Dr Gauld quotes Professor Ian Stevenson who has stated: 'Some 'drop-in' communicators have explained their presence very well and their motivation to communicate is an important part of the whole case which has to be explained as well as the provenance of any information communicated.'

Dr Gauld continues: 'Drop-in' communicators may sometimes represent themselves as wishing to assuage the grief of living friends, as brought along by persons in the next world who have previously communicated through the same medium, as lost in a kind of limbo where the medium is their only means of contact with others, as linked through common interest to persons present, as altruistically trying to help, as simply 'dropping-in' for a chat. It is difficult indeed to decide how seriously the communicators' own explanations of their presences ought to be taken; but sometimes at least the professed explanations are in 'character'.'

Chapter 6

MEDIUMSHIP

Drop-in communicators obviously need to use a medium to get their message across, but let us look at other aspects and evidence gained through mediumship.

In all avenues of psychical research there is always a cross-over from one topic to another, for example an apparition may also cause poltergeist activity. That is why I am not keen on specific definitions as I don't believe that we have the correct vocabulary in dealing with these matters.

One of the 'things that you can do when you're dead' seems to be giving some kind of comfort to those remaining behind. As already mentioned I have been studying these phenomena for nearly 30 years now and the next account is 100% accurate in description.

Because of my jointly published research work, and interest in mediumship and other aspects of the paranormal I am often contacted by people that I do not know. In 1996, a woman contacted me and wanted to talk about the death of her daughter. I duly met her and it became obvious to me that she would have liked me to obtain a sitting with a medium for her. As she had told me that her daughter was murdered some three months earlier, I felt that it was too raw and too soon for that course of action. I asked her to tell me nothing of the events surrounding this death and I suggested that we meet again and I asked her to bring me a sealed envelope in which would be some personal possession of the girl. She agreed. It was my intention to take the envelope to a medium, or mediums and ask them to psychometrise it and in that way perhaps gain some sort of reading from it.

At our next meeting she handed me a sealed brown A5 envelope. I could feel that the envelope was "bumpy" but nothing revealed if it was say a watch or a ring or anything definable. I should also add at this point that I did not know which medium or mediums I would have access to for this task.

I visited a medium, unannounced, and asked, as I placed the envelope on a table, "Can you get anything from this?"

After a blank stare the medium said "Do I have to?" I replied –"yes"

I told him nothing at all about the envelope, why I had it in my possession or the circumstances surrounding it. (I did not know much about the circumstances myself)

Reluctantly, he placed his hand on top of it and, with a surprised look on his face, he immediately said, "I have a girl here with longish dark brown hair" –he hesitated for a second then said – "she was killed!"

"She is telling me that she had two tattoos, one above her left breast, in the form of two hearts intertwined, they are done in red and blue. The other is on the back of her right arm. It is a single rose in red and green.

She lives in a cul de sac, one up on the right. Telling me she misses her four cats". She also gave the name of her partner. I will call him Adam (pseudonym).

At this point the medium was looking at me meaningfully, possibly for some acknowledgment that he was correct, but of course I had no idea if his statements were accurate in any sense and merely shrugged my shoulders. My apprehension grew a little with his next statement.

"She is telling me that she was in prison" – the prison's name was given – "when she was younger." I thought well that's either right or wrong; there is no room for interpretation there. He then said that she had a terminated pregnancy when she was younger.

She is saying, "The newspaper reports were wrong, the description of the clothes that I was found in were all wrong. I was actually wearing a pink top, a grey skirt and ankle boots."

"My photograph was moved from the mantelpiece to the top of the TV today by my mum"

"Adam was the first one to know that I was killed, he phoned my mum"

The medium then gave a description of her attack, which I will not elaborate on, but suffice to say that all of her injuries were reported to be at her back.

She "told" the medium that a green car - possibly a Cavalier and a red Astra were relevant to her death. There were two men involved, a white man about five foot six inches tall and a taller and thinner Asian.

The medium also gave me a specific address in Glasgow, a top floor of a tenement building on the right hand side. With that he said "she's gone"

The total time taken for this delivery was less than 15 minutes.

I had recorded all of this information and now had to find a responsible way of speaking to the mother. I made a list of the statements and an appointment to visit the mother's home, next day, for the first time. Other meetings had been in a neutral setting.

As I entered the lounge I noticed a girl's photo on top of the TV. I said casually "Is this May? (Pseudonym) She said "Yes, I put it there yesterday; it used to be on the mantelpiece."

I then said to her that I had a list of statements made by a medium, but for all I knew they might be absolute nonsense, so I would read them out one by one and I asked her just to say if they were right or wrong. Every statement I read to the mother was absolutely correct. I did not give her the description given of the attack and did not mention the pregnancy, as she may not have known about it. I felt that she had enough to worry about without that statement. It was established later, however, that the girl's injuries were all at her back. I also did not supply her with the address given, the descriptions of the two men or the cars described in the reading.

In total there were 29 individual statements. Twenty-two out of the 29 were absolutely correct, including the descriptions of the positions, shape and colours of the tattoos. She did have four cats. The statements that were considered not correct were in fact not able to be verified due to the fact that I did not give the mother all of the information re pregnancy, address, description of the murder and the description of the men. But these have been considered "wrong" for evaluation purposes.

Simply put, 78% of the information was correct. This was not general information that could apply to anyone, but was specific to the girl in this case. If we consider the information about the tattoos alone, regarding shape, colour and position and remember that neither the medium nor the researcher knew anything at all about the people involved, far less the validity of the information, then this must surely give us considerable pause for thought.

The outcome of this was that it gave the mother great comfort in the thought that her daughter was 'still around' to give her this information.

When a medium gives a reading from an object that is called psychometry.

Psychical researchers of the calibre of Dr. Osty, Dr. Hettinger, Dr.Pagenstecher, Professor Tenhaeff and Professor Bender, studied a large number of psychometrists over many years. If they were not totally mistaken about their subjects, there were psychics who seemed, by holding or touching objects often wrapped up in padded envelopes, to be able to obtain veridical information about the owners of these objects. In delivering this information, the psychometrists sometimes feel themselves 'overshadowed' or in danger of being possessed by the owners, who most often are dead at the time the psychics were asked to see what information they can pick up by holding the objects. In doing so it has been observed that the psychics may also take on some of the physical behaviour of the owner though they have never before met the owner.

I had my first reading from a medium around 1982. This was not employing psychometry, just a face to face reading merely out of curiosity and in the spirit of investigation. As soon as I walked in the woman, who I had never seen before, said to me 'You have never had a reading before.' This was of course true, but she would not have particularly known that. I cannot remember much about the other details about the reading except that she said 'One day you will be speaking to thousands of people about this truth and when you speak - boy will they listen! I won't be here to see that, but I wish that I could.' My silent reaction to this was to think 'What a lot of rubbish' I certainly had no thought, or wish that this should be so and completely forgot about the whole thing.

In 2001, when I was giving a short talk in Glasgow's City Halls as a warm up to an evening of mediumship by Gordon Smith and Mary Armour, I looked out at the 3,000 or so people in the audience and suddenly remembered that woman's statement. I had to mentally apologise.

Mediumship from a distance

An account of mediumship information, from Helen to Petula (Pseudonym)

I had a phone call just after New Year, 2008, from a woman in Lincolnshire who was devastated after the death of her 18 year old son just 6 days earlier, 28th December. She told me that after her son's funeral the next day she would be joining him. I tried to dissuade her from this course of action and told her to stay by the phone and I would get someone to call her back. (At this point I had not a clue as to who I would manage to get) My first choice was Helen Cuthill, a medium who lives in Carnoustie, and, surprisingly, and much to my relief, she answered the phone. I asked her if she would call the woman back. She said to me immediately-"Does this woman also have a girl in spirit?" I had to say that I did not know and would she phone the woman right away. She did and called me back within 40 minutes when she told me some of the statements that she had given the woman. I asked Helen to immediately write down the things that she had said and send the list to me. Reluctantly she did so, and has added at the bottom of this list that there was a lot more that she can't remember. You must remember that I did not know anything about the woman other than she had lost a son.

After the funeral the next day, I did something that I have never done before and I phoned the mother (who was actually feeling much better after Helen's reading) and asked her if she would also make a list of the things that Helen had told her. I said that it may help other grieving parents. She readily agreed that she would do so and I have also received that list.

Helen's statements	Petula's statements
I have a boy here, smiling and laughing and he is saying that he is 'Jack the Lad'.	Son's name is Jack.
He has fair hair and blue eyes.	Strawberry blonde hair and blue eyes.
He is not thin, but he is not big.	Correct description.

You have a girl in spirit also.
Seems to refer to Helen's words to me in
in the original phone call.

Baby girl miscarriage (1994).

He has a big wide smile and a laugh
that stands out.

Mother agrees this description.

It was his lungs, like pneumonia.

It was his lungs, pulmonary
oedema.

Mum was worried that she had given
me too many paracetamol.

Petula did worry about this.

The doctor said no – as it was fluid.

Step dad in spirit with me.

Yes (died 1992).

Mentions a black and white spaniel dog.

Yes – a cocker spaniel
Jemima, Died 2005.

A female cat.

No.

Medium picked up a catholic connection.

Educated in a Catholic school.

Tell mum to spend the money that she
as saved for me.

She had saved money for him
she wanted to get him a car.

Mum wanted to get me a car.

He was training as a welder.

He was training as a welder.

I would have fixed the broken gate in
the garden, but I didn't get a chance.

The garden gate did need fixing.

He is jokingly saying that he was fed
up whistling in the bathroom as
the door jammed and didn't close properly.

The bathroom door had swollen
and does not close properly.

I have a brother.

He has a brother.

He is lazy.

No.

Brother aged 23.	True.
My brother had a dark car – the medium thought that it was dark blue.	True/ish – actually black.
Mentioned Jill, Gill.	True.
My girlfriend is beautiful.	Mum said true.
There will be black horses at my funeral.	True – Wilber and Digby.
My favourite song will be played.	True.
In his coffin he was dressed in a red football strip.	True –Manchester United.
Mum didn't put my boots in.	Correct.
My brother put boots in, but they were old ones not my new ones.	True.
He teased that the brother wanted to keep the boots for himself but his feet were bigger.	True, his feet are a size bigger.
Gave mum the month of her birthday.	True – May.
Gave step dad's birthday, and step dad's month of death.	True June. July (he loved his step dad).
Said that his brother lives in a cul de sac.	On checking with Petula it was established that brother does live in a cul de sac.
Predicted mum would meet a quietly spoken man and that she would have a grand–daughter.	(cant be evaluated)
Described what gran looked like.	Could describe a few people.
Said his granddad liked a bet on the horses.	True

Natural father never around since
he was a baby.

True had not seen him in 17
years but it didn't matter.

Mum has fair hair and about to have
it highlighted and cut (that night).

True.

Step granddad died in hospital.

True (1992).

Granddad liked a drop of whiskey.

True (favourite drink).

Helen also said that Petula would be
putting roses in the coffin – Petula said no,
but on the day of the funeral her estranged
mother came in with three roses in her
hand and walked up and put them
in the coffin.

True.

(Helen, at this point did not know
about the roses going in the coffin.)

Helen mentioned Meg and Margaret –
this is the one person - his natural
Grandmother on his dad's side of the
family.

Also Peg.

His dad's grandmother.

He said that there was a photo of him,
with a flower next to it. Petula's mum
had done this, unknown to her.

He also remarked that he didn't like
how he looked in his coffin.
(due to fluid).

Said he has met Robin.

A neighbour who died in 2004.

Mentioned Bob.

Could be Jack's dog.

Mentioned a white dog.	English bull terrier of the family, died in 1999.
Said he had met David.	Mum not sure who this is.
Said met James.	This was an old fiancé of Petula's who died in 2002.
Met Jamie.	This was a young man who had lived across the road who died in the 1990s – Jack knew him.
He said – "You must go on Mum - not take your life" (can't be evaluated)	

I leave these facts with you and you can make of them what you will. The mother has gone on to become a healer, confident that her son is happy.

So it would appear that the son was able to communicate with his mother and alleviate her pain and suffering after his passing. This is something that he could do after his death and it is interesting to note, in a similar manner to Runki, that he was aware of events on Earth which took place after his passing, namely the roses in the coffin and in Runki's case the deterioration of the rock.

Mediumship in general

In 1982 I began to look at mediumship out of curiosity. I had no bereavement or unhappiness issues at that time. I attended events which would give me the opportunity to see mediums in action. During this phase I witnessed some quite extraordinary information given to people in the audience. With notebook and pen in hand I proceeded to take this further.

The accounts below are some of the early 'messages.' Certainly the circumstances were not 'controlled' but the outcome led me to believe that there was something to be investigated further. This, of course was done in due course in a combined five year research practical study, with Archie Roy, of the information given by mediums in controlled conditions. Over this period we tested a total of 27 mediums in various venues throughout the UK. All of the mediums gave of their time freely as they wanted to assist in any venture that could possibly lead to a further understanding of the processes involved. During the second phase, with the mediums working in conditions up to triple blind, the hypothesis that we were testing was 'All mediums statements are so general that they could be accepted by anyone' After examining the results from this phase of experimentation we concluded that the hypothesis was nullified, with the odds against chance being a million to one.

A few years ago I watched a young medium from Coventry, Darren Britten, give clairvoyance in a church hall at a spiritualist service. The young man had literally come off the Glasgow train prior to going onto the platform to participate in the service. I had heard of him but had never actually seen him work before and my presence was as a researcher. I had my notebook and pen at the ready and wearing my researcher's hat made notes of all of the information given to sitters throughout the service. The standard of information in general seemed quite high – no trivial generalities – but the set of statements made to one young couple was outstanding.

I know for a fact that Darren had never met this couple before yet he told them of their little girl who had died. He did not guess any names but simply said "I have Linda here, she was 9 years old when she passed." He continued to tell of the exact illness which took her and spoke of the amount of money that her parents had raised for that specific charity after her death. He described her last birthday present, which was a bicycle in specific colours and which had pink ribbons coming out of the handles. He then informed the lady that Linda liked the shoes that she had bought that day and told her of the exact amount of money that she had paid for them. No piece of information was wrong. The proceedings were carried out in such a happy manner that the parents did not know whether to laugh or cry, but I certainly had my handkerchief out.

Another medium who provides consistently evidential information at all of the services at which he officiates is Gordon Smith. Some time ago I watched him give three ladies a message about a young man who had died tragically. He gave the young man's name, the location of his death, his grandmother's full name and wished one of the ladies good luck in her job interview the following Wednesday. He finished by telling her that there were to be legal repercussions concerning his death but allayed any fears that the family may have had about his passing by telling them that he felt no pain as it was just like going to sleep and wakening up again. On many occasions I have heard him describe in detail the necklace being worn under a blouse or jumper around the neck of the recipient. This is usually followed by the recipient hauling out the chain or necklace for all to see as it is displayed to the assembled people. I have also heard him inform people that they have a newspaper cutting in a handbag or wallet with a photograph of a specific person in that cutting. Often he also provides the date of the newspaper cutting and the recipient has to check to see if that is correct. It has always been correct, even when the recipient was unaware of the exact date before looking.

I was at a public demonstration of mediumship in a spiritualist church in Glasgow, where the medium demonstrating was from Birmingham. During this demonstration I witnessed some of the best evidence I have heard given in such circumstances. The medium was a real "Brummy" and the recipient concerned very Glaswegian, indeed and even I had a problem understanding some of her responses. When the medium came to the recipient and the two females next to her they were very unresponsive and would hardly give a shrug of the shoulders or a nod of the head. The medium issued statements; she did not ask any questions.

She said

"There is a boy sitting here on the platform swinging his legs. He looks about 6 years of age—and he is looking for his mum."

Response from the audience—zero—none—not a sound.

The medium then pointed up the centre aisle to a girl, about 10 rows back who appeared to be with another two females, and said;

"You are his mum." The girl nodded but did not speak.

Medium; "His name is Steven." The girl nodded but did not speak.

" He died of a broken neck." The girl nodded but did not speak

"He is writing up 11 for me, therefore he would be 11 years old if he was here now." The girl nodded as before.

"He is showing me a rope and he is swinging from a tree,—it is as though the rope broke or something and he fell down"

Recipient; "We don't know if there was a rope or not, but he did fall from a tree and broke his neck"

The medium then pointed to the lady two along from the girl and said "You are his Gran, he is telling me that" This lady looked too young to be anybody's Gran and it would have been very unlikely that the medium could have guessed this. The lady nodded.

Medium; "He is telling me that you were looking through old photos of him today"

The lady nodded in affirmation.

To the mother she then imparted; "I never got to wear the new trainers you bought me." At this the mother and gran reacted by bringing out the hankies, and so did I.

The mother then explained aloud about the trainers, but I could not entirely understand what she was saying.

Medium; to the three females " He is handing me a large carton of popcorn"

The three ladies then laughed aloud, while dabbing their eyes, as this was seemingly his favourite snack.

The medium then laughed and said that he had gone saying "I'm away now" and that he had cut off communication, which is entirely consistent in my experience with the behaviour of a small boy.

My point is this, that if all mediumistic information was as definite as this then there would be no question in the mind of the general public that good mediums do transfer relevant information. On this occasion the accuracy of the information and the method in which it was relayed was outstanding and left the audience, many of who were there for the first time, with plenty to think about.

Note for us all: keep accentuating the positive!

Helen Cuthill, a medium from the north of Scotland, also impresses me very much. The first time I witnessed her demonstrating her talent was at a weekend conference for which I was the organiser. The conference was away from my home town and certainly well away from hers. The delegates at the conference were unknown to myself and any of the other speakers or demonstrators, as the bookings had been made through a third party, who did not even know the medium's name; I make this point in case anyone wishes to label the events as collusion. Once again I was recording the information given by the medium as she demonstrated. The first lady whom she came to was a complete stranger, and a very quiet lady, in fact when Helen spoke to her she was not a helpful recipient at all in the sense that she would not even answer yes or no, she just kind of grudgingly, barely, nodded her head. Her first words were "I have your son here", she gave his name, just one name, not a choice, and other personal details only for his mother's understanding and a clear indicator that he had an insight into the everyday workings of his mother's life. She then told the lady that her mother was "here" and described her in great detail giving a specific hairstyle, height, the type of spectacles she wore and other personal details. Other communicators were brought for this lady, all very relevant, and I have to add that after that weekend conference, the recipient looked much more relaxed and happier than when she arrived.

The next recipient of a communicator was an elderly gentleman, a very bright and intelligent man, who had travelled quite a distance to this conference. Helen brought his wife to him, giving her name and other details, but the interesting thing was that she said that his wife and his mother were coming in arm in arm like mother and daughter; the man laughed and said that this would be correct as she just loved his wife as if she was a real daughter and not just a daughter-in-law. How many of us love our in-laws in this way? If you want to say that this was a guess it was an exceptionally good one. If you want to say that it is telepathy, that is also your choice, but it is still paranormal in the sense that the ordinary senses would not yield this type of information. During ordinary telepathy tests Helen just showed average ability. However mediums would not rule out the possibility that they have some kind of telepathic link with those who have passed on.

Speaking of normally accepted means, even the respected magazine The New Scientist recently published an article about "blind sight" in which they accept the results of tests carried out by scientists on a person with sight in one eye and none in the other. They have established, without any doubt, that the person can distinguish colours held behind his head, at the blind side. They admit that they do not understand the mechanisms involved, but can testify that it is a fact. Perhaps it's just my thinking but that sounds jolly like empirical results in psychical research to me.

A general misconception is that all mediums charge a fortune for their services, this is simply not the case. Historically, the very good mediums who agreed to be studied gave of their time freely. One example of this was John Sloan, the medium whom Arthur Findlay studied. He willingly allowed and encouraged Arthur Findlay to join with his home circle and welcomed everyone with open arms and yet when this man actually died, he was buried in very meagre circumstances.

It is my experience, and the experience of my colleagues, that modern sensitives are more than happy to work with psychical researchers, with no thought of payment whatsoever. They are delighted to help with experimentation. Mediums themselves are interested and curious as to the possible mechanisms involved in their mediumistic gift. Every medium to whom I have spoken has stated that they do not understand "how", i.e. by what means, they are able to "see", "hear" or "sense" a deceased person, only that they can. A medium has to stand on a platform and trust that he/she will receive information to pass on to a sitter. I have never yet met a medium who is not nervous, to some extent, before a public meeting. A normally good medium, who may not be in receptive mood, may at some point in time receive nothing to express. I have actually seen this happen, and the honest response is to tell the audience that he/she is receiving nothing and sit down. I have also seen this done and I feel that this action has to be applauded. This is where, in my opinion, people err in trying to perform a sole demonstration of these talents in, for example, a large theatre. If they are not receiving anything there must be an enormous pressure to cold guess or give out generalities as the audience have paid for their tickets and no-one would want to send them home. This does not mean that this person cannot receive, and transmit, good evidential communications, merely that that facility is not working at that particular time and under these specific conditions.

If they are honest, as I said earlier, the question that most people ask themselves at some time in their lives is;

"Is there any possibility that we may, in some way, survive physical death?" I can remember even as a young child, asking myself that question. Surely this topic is of the utmost importance to each and every one of us, and the reason why people study the subject in the hope of gaining hard evidence.

Sadly, the public in general do not realise that serious investigators, mostly from a hard scientific background, study the paranormal, which I would describe as an event or a series of events which cannot be explained within normally accepted scientific paradigms. All aspects of the paranormal have been studied through the years and mediums and mediumship in particular have come in for much attention. This has always been the case. In days gone by:

Sir William Crookes the world-renowned chemist, studied Florence Cook and Daniel Dunglas Home.

F.W.H.Myers wrote about the subject in *Human Personality and its Survival Of Bodily Death.*

Sir Oliver Lodge studied the mediums of the time, Mrs Willett and Mrs Leonard.

Professor William James studied Mrs Leonora Piper.

Charles Richet, Nobel prize winner, studied Eusapia Palladino, as did The Honorable Everard Feilding, a gentleman who was also a conjurer, and who might have been expected to have detected a fraud if it had been present.

Harry Price studied the Scottish medium Helen Duncan, a medium who was able to give the names of young men who had perished in the Second World War and the circumstances of their deaths even before their relatives had been notified.

Among others, as already mentioned in this book, was Major Oliver Villiers who studied the information given by Eileen Garrett, an Irish born medium. Many notables and clergy studied Ena Twigg, in fact Bishop Pike wrote a book full of high praise about his experiences with her.

Arthur Findlay, a wealthy stockbroker and businessman, as already stated, studied John Sloan over many years and became the author of many books on the subject, including *Looking Back*, *The Rock of Truth*, *The Edge of The Etheric*, and *The Way of Life*.

All of the above had nothing to gain by investigating their subjects, except experience and the furtherance of their own knowledge regarding the position of human beings upon this earth. Each of the above worked openly and honestly, with perhaps the exception of Harry Price, who latterly appeared to be affected by the "politics" of the time.

The list could go on and on.

So what is the response of the hardened sceptic to all of the work which has been carried out in the past; the range is usually one of the following.

We know that these things cannot happen; therefore all of these people are stupid and are being fooled. Shades of "the earth is flat, everyone knows that."

Their methods are sloppy or flawed.

People are hearing and seeing what they wish to hear and see.

People are being deliberately tricked.

They are all telling lies or cheating.

A magician could do the same.

These people are just those spiritualist people who believe in it.

Where is their evidence that this is so in all cases?

The medium Daniel Dunglas Home, for example, displayed massive paranormal gifts, witnessed by many, but he himself never actually associated himself with the spiritualist movement, although he did study it and was the authored a book on the subject, *Lights and Shadows of Spiritualism*.

Lord Adare published a book entitled, *Experiences in Spiritualism with D. D. Home* about his experiences with DD Home. Adare was not a spiritualist either, but in the company of three other notable people had conversations with deceased persons through the trance mediumship of Home. NO blackout conditions were imposed, everyone could see quite clearly during all of the proceedings. The sheer quantity and quality of his phenomena seem to be unsurpassed to this day, and in actual fact all of his phenomena were exhibited in good conditions of light. Lord Adare studied Home for some time, resulting as indicated earlier in the publication of a book on the subject. I now quote the following from that book as published in *The Occult* by Colin Wilson.

> "Spirits appeared as dim shapes, and sometimes as walking clouds; draughts howled through the room when all doors and windows were closed; doors opened and closed; flowers fell from the ceiling; spirit hands appeared; furniture moved around as though it was weightless. Home himself floated around like a balloon. He floated out of one window head first - it was only open one foot - and returned through another window. He would elongate, standing against a wall, while one man held his feet, another his waist, and another watched his face. Homes height would then increase from five feet ten to six feet six inches, both heights being marked on the wall."

Adare's book was privately printed, but caused so much commotion that it was withdrawn"

In 1872 Home agreed to be studied by Sir William Crookes, the well-respected chemist of the time. No doubt the scientific "establishment" thought that this would be the ultimate exposure and Home would be proved to be a fake. After studying D.D. Home for some time, Crookes was totally convinced that his feats were genuine, including all of those reported earlier in this chapter, as he too had witnessed similar phenomena. In case you are thinking that perhaps Crookes had lost the plot by this time, he continued in his other scientific work during this period and was greatly respected for his further contributions to the study of chemistry so much so that he was then awarded the Order of Merit, knighted by Queen Victoria and elected as the President of the Royal Society. I believe that this attests to his credibility as an honourable witness and to the esteem in which he was held by his peers and all others around him.

Crookes also examined the mediumship of Florence Cook, with whom the critics 'implied' that he was infatuated. They did not mention that Mrs Crookes attended every séance with him. Maybe they thought that he had a crush on Home as well!

Incidentally, when D.D. Home was asked "how" he achieved any of the incredible phenomena which he displayed, he simply said that he did not know, there was no secret, things happened when he made himself relax. It is also worth stressing that he never took one penny from anyone throughout his lifetime in payment for the demonstration of his talents.

Also, regarding the "methodology" of mediumship, the medium Ena Twigg has been quoted in the book *Ena Twigg: Medium* as relating her first experience on a public platform as follows;

"I felt as though my hair was sprouting a tangle of electric wires that were attached to some invisible master switchboard near the ceiling. When a message came through the switchboard the signal tugged at one of the wires pulling my scalp. Then the current connected with the intended recipient. When the right person was found there was a click and I knew that this was correct". After visiting holy places of all religions she said of her reaction to these "I vibrated like a violin string as impressions of the past played upon my sensitivity."

Her definition of mediumship was "sensitiveness", the ability to register vibrations, radiations or frequencies which cannot be captured by any of the five senses.

These things happen. If you have not had experience of them then do not dismiss them out of hand until you have carried out some kind of experimentation, research or fact finding mission. It should go without saying that good researchers just want to find out the truth of these matters. Perhaps one reason why the present day genuine mediums enjoy co-operating with good psychical researchers is in the hope that we all may eventually provide a scientific template for perfect conditions which would enable mediums to produce the best evidence that they can at all times.

Wouldn't that be good; we live in hope!

Albert Einstein said that 'All propositions arrived at without experience are devoid of reality.'

This would indeed seem to be the case.

Chapter 7

REINCARNATION

Another 'thing' that at least some people appear to be able to do when they are dead is to return to Earth as another physical being. There are thousands of cases of children who remember a previous life. Professor Ian Stevenson from the University of Virginia, and his department, have collected nearly 3000 such cases and are in the process of putting them into a data base. Although a good number of these cases are from Eastern countries, they are certainly not all. Any time that I give a talk on reincarnation, someone usually comes up to me at the end and shares an account from within his/her own family. I have to say that people do not like this idea as they feel that their children do not really belong to 'them.' To expand on this idea would take forever, but just know that that person has chosen to come into your life and, where there is love, that bond will never be broken, regardless of personality. Here is one example.

Cameron

A boy who remembers a previous life on the island of Barra, Scotland.

He was born near Glasgow on 23rd August, 2000. Mary Rose Barrington, of The Society for Psychical Research, asked me to investigate the case of ostensible reincarnation of Cameron as the family home is within easy distance of Glasgow. Professor Archie Roy accompanied me on most my visits to this family. I have video recordings of all of the interviews and these are date stamped.

Ever since Cameron could speak with any clarity, he spoke frequently to his family about having lived on Barra, where the aeroplanes landed on the sand. Initially his mother paid little or no attention to this thinking that it was a fantasy.

Cameron has an older brother, Mark, (pseudonym) who is 13 months older than him.

His mother, Norma, says that it was just like bringing up twins; they did everything together as they were so close in age. Cameron used to speak to his brother about Barra constantly, so much so that the brother would yell in despair, "Gonnie shut up about Barra" He used to say to Norma "You've only got one toilet in this house, in Barra we had three." He never changed his story. He said to Norma "You would like my Barra Mum, she's nice, and we could go and see her" He said it with such affection. He spoke about living in a white house and being able to see the beach from his bedroom window as it looked on to the beach and that the sheep used to come up to the front door of the house. He said that there were boxes outside the house, where he thought that fish was kept.

He gave details of the family group. He had three brothers and three sisters. "They were allowed to go and play on the beach on their own but I had to have someone with me." He spoke about playing with a black and white dog and often referred to a big black car and the fact that there were always plenty of children around to play with. He never referred to his own name, but said that his father was called Shane, and said that his father had stepped out onto a road and was knocked down by a car. He also said that he was with him when this happened. (We have no information if this happened in Barra, Glasgow or elsewhere).

When Norma asked him about his mother's name he replied "She was called Mummy" a response delivered with a kind of scathing look. He enthusiastically told Norma that his Barra Mum has long hair down to "there" as he pointed to below his waist and then he added, "but she got it cut shorter". He kept saying "You'll like her Mum when you see her, when we go to Barra. Please can we go? You'll like her." Cameron had no religious upbringing of any kind and Norma herself said that if we had asked her two years ago if she actually believed in reincarnation, she would have said "Definitely not." He was only about 4 when he spoke about the telephone in this house being different to the one in Barra. He said that it was big and black with holes in it, and, as he spoke, he made an old fashioned dialling motion as though using an old fashioned telephone. In fact he gave himself the name "Barra Boy". For non-Scots a "Barra boy" in Scotland is one who pushes a wheelbarrow. Even Cameron could see the humour in this.

He said that he used to go out and play in rock pools and catch crabs. He said that he loved doing that and he could even swim in some of the pools. He said to Norma earlier in his life "These houses are very close together, where I was before there was loads of space to run around the outside of the house; no one else was right beside us" When she asked what his name was he said "The Robertsons owned the house and I was part of the family" (I thought that this was a strange thing to say). "They lived in Glasgow and the house was a holiday home."

He used to plead with his family "Take me to Barra and you'll see it's true." He used to get annoyed with Norma because she didn't know about his other mum. Tears would run down his face and he would say "My other family are missing me!" He fell at nursery a couple of years ago and wanted his Barra Mum to pick him up. Norma thought, "Why does he not want me to be his Mum?" She has often sat in tears over this. She asked him one time how he "got" here and the reply was that "I was with my Barra Mum and then I fell through a hole and I was with you" His friend next door is called Alan (pseudonym) and one day the mother of this child came in to Norma and said that this was getting out of hand as Cameron had told Alan "Don't worry about it if you die you can come back as somebody else." Another time, just out of the blue he said to Norma "See when you die, cause you'll go first and then me and Mark will die, we've to wait for a woman that's going to have three children and we've to come back and you'll be our sister and not our Mum"

In 2006, a little girl, Debbie (pseudonym), from Cameron's school was knocked down by a car and killed. Mark came home from school very upset and Norma was trying to console him when Cameron said "I don't know why you're getting upset, she's got a choice." Norma asked what he meant. In a very matter of fact tone he announced "She's got a choice whether she stays where she is or comes back." The brother Mark has never spoken about any former life, despite listening to Cameron through the years. Cameron's friend Alan, who lives next door, said to his mother years ago "It's funny that Cameron has two Mummies and I only have one.

When Cameron attended nursery school he spoke about Barra the whole time to his teacher and one time when they were all going in a taxi Cameron said to the driver "Take me to Barra." When he had to go for his pre-school jabs to the health visitor, he said to her "I don't need them I had my jabs done in Barra." Norma blanched and had to explain about the whole thing. Norma said that no matter the truth the whole thing was real to Cameron, he regularly used to sit with tears running down his face, saying "take me to Barra." The health visitor contacted a psychologist who said "Don't worry about it" When he was at school Norma would try to help him with his homework and he would say "I know how to do it, I did it in Barra" Norma has persevered in asking him the names of his brothers and sisters, but he keeps saying "I can't remember." Norma thought that this was strange, because if he was making the whole thing up he would surely make up the names of the brothers and sisters.

As the Mum and Dad had by this time split up, a trip to Barra was out of the question as the cost was prohibitive in itself. Cameron spoke constantly to all of his friends and neighbours about being in Barra. Initially Norma did not know where Barra was and had to look it up in a map. In 2006 a friend of theirs, actually the nursery teacher noticed an advert in a local paper for people who felt that they had lived before to come forward and tell their story. Norma contacted the paper, against the advice of her brother and father, and from that point things escalated way beyond any expectation that she may have had. The staff at Cameron's school was also not pleased. However she felt that if Cameron spoke about it to a stranger that it might stop the constant appeal to go to Barra.

The local paper then became involved with a television company, October films, who then took the case on board. Dr Jim Tucker from the University of Virginia was contacted over this matter. He is a protégé of the aforementioned Professor Ian Stevenson, who has investigated claims of ostensible past lives over a period of over 40 years. The film company decided to take the family to Barra.

As they were preparing to board the plane to Barra, Norma said to Cameron "If you are telling lies, now is the time to speak up. He replied no, no I'm not, and I'll show you where I used to go - what I used to do." He said to Norma "When we get to Barra, they won't know you, but they'll be nice to you, but they'll know me – I'm from Barra".

On the plane he said to his mum "Is my face red and shiny?"

Reply "Why would your face be red and shiny?"

Reply "Because I'm happy."

As they left the plane he said "I told you it was real, I told you it was true." Norma was surprised to see that the plane really did land on the beach, as Cameron had said; she had assumed that it would clear the beach and land on a proper runway. Awaiting the mini bus to take them to the hotel Cameron pointed in one direction and said "I used to play over there." They then were driven over part of the island for about half an hour, Cameron made no comment on the houses as they passed, except for one where he pointed and said "I know the people who live there (then a pause) but I can't remember their names." He made no claim to see his "Barra" house. Upon reaching the hotel Cameron was as high as a kite and kept saying "I'll show you tomorrow, I'll show you where I swam in the rock pools." Norma was not convinced that this would be the case. On the first day the research team had visited a local Historian who informed them that there were no, nor had been, Robertsons on the island.

On the second day they received a telephone call from the historian to say that there had been a holiday house owned by Robertsons in the 1960's and 70's. It was on the other side of the island. He had obviously thought about it and loosened the innate aversion to "strangers" that seems to be inbuilt in some communities. The research team was able to obtain keys for this house and they all set off. Obviously they did not share this information with Cameron. As they drove towards their destination Cameron suddenly pointed and shouted "You can go out there, but you might need to swim to get back." They were passing a stretch of water with an old ruined building not far off shore. This proved to be correct as the height of water was subject to tidal movement, and at some times in the day you could walk out to the ruin. As they turned down a track road Cameron pointed and said "That's it, that's my house there." Martin's response was "How can that be your house?" The reply was "'Cause that was the Robertson's house and I was part of the family." It was indeed a white house in its own ground. As they got to the gate of the house Norma looked at Cameron and saw that the colour had faded from his face. She said "Are you alright?" The reply was "I'm happy but I'm scared". Norma asked him "Do you want to go into the house?" Reply "Yes." Before they went in they walked around the outside of the property and as they walked Cameron said "There's a bit round here that we called the secret way to the beach" and as they rounded the corner there was a concealed entrance which Cameron pointed out to Norma. He also pointed out the rock pools and some of them were quite large. They later established that in the summer, children do swim in these pools. Returning to the front gate, Mark announced that he did not want to go in, but Cameron said to him "Come on in, you can play with my stuff."

Mark came in. Cameron changed as soon as he walked in the front door, he knew where he was going and the conversation was peppered with phrases such as " This is my room where I slept with my brothers". "This is my sisters' room". He navigated the narrow corridors of the house easily to show Norma the three toilets. As soon as they stepped into the Barra house, Norma said to him "Come and show me up the stairs" She said this as the house looked as though it had an upstairs. Cameron looked at her sideways and replied disdainfully "Don't be silly - there's no upstairs" and, of course, he was correct. Cameron said that the house had changed and indeed it had as through the years bits had been added on.

After the initial excitement, Norma noticed that Cameron seemed a bit flat and she said to him "Did you think your mum would be here?" His response for the camera was to shake his head indicating no, but when they came out he said to Norma "I did think that my family would be there." When they reached the hotel that night Norma asked him how he was feeling and the reply was "I'm happy, but I'm sad."
Incidentally, Norma noted boxes, which were similar to fish boxes in the entrance, but they contained boots and shoes.

The next day he filled his pockets with shells and sand to bring back to Glasgow. He was looking forward to coming back to tell everyone that it was "real." He told the neighbours "Yes, I saw my house and where I used to play – why is everybody going on about it?"

After the visit to Barra the TV people then located a Grace (pseudonym) Robertson who lived in Glasgow and whose family had a holiday home in Barra. They took Cameron to visit her, but the night before the visit Cameron went into a very strange mood and said to his mum "What if she was a wee girl when I was a wee boy? - in a tone of great apprehension"

Norma, herself thought that this was surely a remarkably mature remark for a child of 6 years of age. Grace showed them pictures of the house and it was just the way Cameron had best remembered it, as against the actual modern Barra home where things had been changed slightly. Cameron seemed to be giving the pictures a good scrutiny and when asked what he was doing he said "I'm looking to see if I see me." Norma noted that although the Robertsons owned the house they had caretakers in when they were not there. There was a photograph of the caretakers standing outside the Barra home hanging in Grace's house and in the photograph is a black and white dog, a big black car and loads of children. There was also another photograph where the sheep were in the garden of the home, almost up to the front door. (When the documentary was shown on television they had inserted old footage of two boys on the beach at Barra and when Cameron saw that he said to Norma "Is that me?").

It is not when Cameron is bored that he speaks about Barra. They were at the theatre watching "Joseph" and Cameron was singing along, quite happily, and he turned to Norma and made another reference to Barra.

After the Barra trip, they were at the cinema watching "Chicken Little" when Cameron turned to Norma and said "I know how that chicken felt, nobody believed me either." Through the years Norma has also noticed that from time to time, with regards to food, Cameron will say things like "I never used to like that in Barra, but I like it now" Another time they were on holiday abroad with Norma's sister and her husband, playing in and around the swimming pool and having a laugh when Cameron announced "When I was with my Barra family we never came to anywhere like this." Mark sighed and said "not again!," "Mummy why does he say that?" Norma had to say that she didn't know. But after they all went to Barra Mark said to Norma "Mummy, how does he know all these things?"

Norma informed me that she has had no other men in her life since the boys' father left, and she thought is strange that Cameron said that after his Barra father died, a man came to visit the house and "He said that he was my uncle, but he wasn't. He was like my dad, but not my dad." Norma thought even then "Where is all of this coming from?" Norma is a very honest and uncomplicated person.

Cameron still hates having a bath, it is a major issue. Since visiting Barra, Cameron's attitude has changed, he is more relaxed about it and says "Isn't it funny, when I wanted to speak about Barra nobody wanted to listen and now everybody is talking about it and I'm not bothered. I've nothing to prove any more " Norma said that he was so anxious that people believed him that that was why he was lifting handfuls of Barra sand and trying to put it in his pockets to bring back to Glasgow.

Other witnesses who can testify to the fact that Cameron spoke about Barra from an early age include: Ian Watson, Cameron's uncle, who lives in England. He recollects that from when Cameron could speak he spoke about living in Barra; Ian thought that he meant Barrow in Furness, but Cameron said no, it was an island. He remembers him speaking about, among other things, the house, the three toilets and the rock pools. What impressed Ian over the years was the consistency of Cameron's story and he kept thinking to himself "How has he even heard about Barra?"

On the 15th April 2007 I spoke to the mother of Alan, the boy next door to Cameron. Her name is Ann Millar(pseudonym). She confirmed that Cameron has been talking about Barra for as long as she can remember. When Alan used to say to her " How come Cameron has two Mums and I only have one" or "How come Cameron has two houses and I only have one" she would play it down and say "He's making it up, it's just a story." But, quote "When it all turned out to be correct, I had some explaining to do!"

Brother Mark has changed his mind about Cameron. When I spoke to him he said "At first I didn't believe him, but now I do"

I asked Cameron what the weather was like in Barra and the reply was "Wet and rainy" I asked him what he did in the rock pools and he said "Playing in the rock pools, catching little things in the rock pools."

I asked Cameron what is the last thing that he remembered about Barra and he replied "I was lying in bed."

He had previously said that he "fell through" into Norma's tummy. I asked him what it was like when he "Fell through" and he said "Like bungee jumping."

It is noted that he has a small scar just above his buttocks, but at this time no relevance can be attached to this.

In July 2007 the family were on holiday abroad with another family and at the beach Cameron announced "If we were all on Barra, I'd be older than any of you"

Cameron is now beginning to forget some of the information he had previously given about Barra. He said to me "Sometimes it is hard to remember."

In the TV documentary about Cameron, you can actually see a big black car which looked like the one that he had spoken about, ever so fleetingly, in the photograph album that Grace Robertson is holding.

I am still looking for a contact in Barra who might know the name of the housekeepers in 1960's/70's.

Most children who remember a previous life tend to forget it after the age of 6/7, but the next case is quite different.

Purnima

Professor Erlendur Haraldsson first met Purnima and her parents in September 1996, at her home in Bakamuna, Sri Lanka. She was nine years old at the time and still spoke of her previous life. Haraldsson remarks that in such cases this was unusual because most children stop doing so around the age of five or six. Her father was the principal of a secondary school and her mother was a schoolteacher. Purnima made a very favourable impression on the psychical researcher, being well adjusted and happy in her family; she communicated with him freely and on occasion corrected her parents' statements. She had an excellent school record and altogether was an intelligent, beautiful and charming girl.

Originally, when she began to speak of past events in 1990, her parents paid little attention; it was not until early in 1993 that they took some interest in what she said and made an attempt to follow it up. Being quite westernised, they had no immediate thoughts of reincarnation.

As a small child Purnima made a number of child–like remarks to her mother about 'people who drive over other people' being very bad and also mentioned a fatal accident with a big vehicle (her Sri Lankan words mean bus or truck). Purnima's mother was upset when a traffic accident happened near their home. Purnima tried to soothe her mother by saying "Do not think about the accident, I came to you after such an accident." This in itself is a highly unusual statement for a young child to make, although there may be a parallel in the previous account in Scotland.

Purnima also gave an account of how she died in the accident and how she then found herself floating in the air in semi darkness for some days. She 'Saw people moaning and crying and saw her body up to and including the funeral. There were many people like me floating around. I then saw some light, went there, and came "here" (to Bakamuna).'

The information she gave about types of incense, naming them, describing in detail how different types are created, was completely beyond a child of that age's experience. She indicated that she also oversaw the production of incense. It is a measure of her parents' reluctance to accept her statements that they made attempts to account for he names Ambiga and Geta Pichcha incense by checking the shops in Bakamuna, finding only two kinds of incense made in Kandy and one from India, none of these was Ambiga or Gita Pichcha.

About the age of four, Purnima saw a TV programme about the Kelaniya temple, close to Colombo and about 145 miles from Bakamuna.

She said that she recognised the temple. Later, and before she entered school, she was allowed to accompany a group of schoolchildren, in the charge of her parents, on a visit to Kelaniya temple. While in Kelaniya she said she had lived on the other side of the Kelaniya river, which flows beside the temple compound.

In 1995 W E Sumanasiri, a graduate from Kelaniya University, was appointed to teach in Bakamuna and he and Purnima's father became acquainted. They agreed that Sumanasiri, who still lived in Kelaniya at the weekends, where he had married, would make inquiries across the Kelaniya River. Haraldsson carefully states that Sumanasiri did not meet Purnima until after his inquiries. He also lists the items that Purnima's father gave the graduate to check. Among many statements were the following:

> 1 She had lived on the other side of the river from the Kelaniya Temple
> 2 She had been making Ambiga and Geta Pichcha incense sticks
> 3 She was selling incense sticks on a bicycle
> 4 She had a fatal accident with a big vehicle

During the visit to Kelaniya, in March 1993, Sumanasiri was accompanied in his enquiries by his brother-in-law, Tony Serasinghe Modalige, a native of Kelaniya and another local person. They involved themselves in a thorough search leading from the information given by Purnima. They found three incense makers, all small family businesses. One of them named his brands Ambiga and Geta Pichcha. The owner, L A Wijisere, had a brother-in-law and associate named Jinadasa Perera, who had died (In September 1995) in an accident with a bus as he was bringing incense to the market on a bicycle. They also found that Wijisere's and Jinadasa's house and factory had been 2.4 miles from the ferry and 5-10 minutes walking distance from the Kelaniya River.

The visit to Wijisiri family was very brief. Sumansiri told Purnima's father of his findings. It was the following month when Purnima, her parents, Sumansiri and his brother-in-law made an unannounced visit to the Wijisiri home in Angoda. Before going to Angoda they spent a night at Sumansiri's home. According to Purnima's mother, Purnima whispered to her: "This incense dealer [me] had two wives. This is a secret, don't give them my address – they might trouble me."

When the group first arrived at Wijisiri's house, he was absent but returned a short time later. As he approached the house Purnima said;

"This is Wijisiri, he is my brother-in-law." During the visit she alone, of the visitors, spoke. The householder was puzzled when she said she wanted to see her brother-in-law and sister. Actually Wijisiri didn't want anything to do with her at all until he actually listened to what she was saying.

Realisation dawned that this little girl was referring to a previous life and he was most surprised when she began asking technical questions about various kinds of incense packets. Indeed she asked and discussed with him all kinds of topics about the production, packaging and marketing of incense sticks. She talked about an accident that Wijisiri himself had and she asked, by name, about various friends of Jinadasa. She also asked about her mother and her precious sister.

Purnima then showed him her birthmarks. According to Haraldsson, after her birth, her mother noticed a cluster of hypo-pigmented birth marks to the left of the midline of her chest and over her lower ribs. Purnima stated "This is the mark received when I was hit by a bus." She also named the place where the accident happened. The medical evidence concerning Jinadasa's fatal injuries in the accident is undeniable. Professor Haraldsson was told by Jinadasa's brother that he and his sister were called into the mortuary to identify the body. He told Haraldsson that he had seen massive injuries from the lower ribs on the left hand side and up and obliquely across the body. Indeed Haraldsson obtained the detailed post-mortem report from the physician, Dr Karijawasam, who conducted the post-mortem. The rib fractures were listed by number, the liver and spleen were ruptured and the lungs were penetrated by the broken ribs. Externally there was a grazed abrasion 23 inches by 10 inches, running obliquely from the right shoulder across the chest to the left lower abdomen.

She also stated that they had moved their home and factory within Angoda from the time she was with them. All of this was correct.

It transpired that Jinadasa did, in fact, have two wives although he had never formally married either of them.

After the two families met, Purnima made some interesting statements about Jinadasa's life with his first wife that she could hardly have learnt from anyone. With no way of verifying some of these they have to be listed among the indeterminate items. Haraldsson states that Purnima's checkable statements could not be faulted. Indeed it would appear that as in many such cases, beyond the hard 'checkable' statements that are correct, there are many remarks made by the child that are considered 'indeterminate' that is, taken by themselves would be seized upon by a sceptical person as 'cold reading', 'the Barnum effect' or derived from 'body language.' But this is a child who provided many absolutely correct statements about a life that she could not have conceivably encountered. The constellations of indeterminate statements, in my opinion, must surely act as an additional 'bundle of twigs' each perhaps, according to a sceptic, weak, but together forming a strong support to the formidable evidential structure provided by the child's verifiable statements.

Like many such cases, although the child provides many correct statements about his or her former life before the former family is tracked down and the first visit is made, the first visit seems to trigger many more memories. Just as in this life if we revisit a place after many years, that visit then triggers memories that may have lain dormant in us since our original visit, all those years ago. In ostensible reincarnation cases this is more so if the child meets people he or she knew in that former life. They often comment on; changes made to the house since he or she knew it; recognitions of people, where sometimes the errors are important as in addressing a woman by her maiden name when in fact she was married after the previous person died. These phenomena in such cases can be disconcerting to witnesses.

Why the previous personality appears to have come back in the form of Purnima, who knows? Professor Haraldsson classifies the case of Purnima as a good example of a case with different characteristics that fall into a pattern and must be viewed as a whole considering memories, birthmarks and practical knowledge relating to the previous life. Overall, he adds, one can state that the case of Purnima Ekanayake is of unusual quality.

I thoroughly agree. Taking into consideration the 40 years' work by Professor Ian Stevenson I remain baffled at the inability of the scientific establishment to make the paradigm shift and accept that the main task is no longer the collection and study of more cases, as the records number nearly 3,000 at present, but to study the evidence, compare the data features and finally understand what the children are telling the world about fundamental features of the nature of human personality and possible survival of bodily death.

Obviously it is tempting to advance reincarnation as the most plausible theory to account for such cases though Stevenson himself was always very careful to avoid any dogmatic assertion that reincarnation is the explanation. Reincarnation of course is a version of the survival theory. The soul or spirit may live on earth more than once and although it would appear that few people ever recall details of a previous life that is not to say that they have not had one. In Stevenson's database there are certainly many verified cases showing that such fascinating aspects of human personality do occur. An examination has shown that where the previous life was cut short by violence, the time interval between the death of the previous life and the birth of the child is significantly shorter than that between the normal death at a mature age and the birth of the child

I had not personally given the concept of reincarnation a lot of thought until a friend of long standing had an unusual experience with her small son. The household concerned had no preconceived ideas, or even an interest, in the topic of reincarnation before the event occurred; therefore no external influences were brought to bear in the form of any preconditioning before the following account. When her son was approximately three and a half years of age he came into the kitchen from playing in the back garden; the usual colour of such a boy, covered in grime from head to toe. My friend caught him in transit on his way through the kitchen in order that she might wash his face and hands at least before he ate his dinner. She took him back towards the kitchen sink to wipe off the rough dirt with a cloth and perhaps she did not have the gentlest of touches.

He suddenly jumped back, holding a hand to one side of his head and said in a serious manner "Don't rub me there - that's where I died!" He looked straight into her face with eyes wide open and with an expressionless face. Her first instinct was to say "Don't be so silly" but she did not. After a pause in her mental processes she said something like "Oh - tell me about it." The child told of the last mummy and daddy he had who hit him, and who eventually threw him out of a window resulting in him landing on his head where he sustained injury from which he never recovered. Then in a matter of fact tone he stated "That is why I chose to come to a Mummy and Daddy this time who would love me." Without a change in the tone of his voice the next sentence was something like, now what's for tea?

My friend was speechless and did not know what to make of this at all, but was aware that the child was speaking seriously. Now if this was the only account of an event such as this one could fairly happily dismiss it as a very advanced fantasy, albeit there was no denying the sincerity of the child when speaking to his mother. But we receive and have investigated similar accounts to this given by other children, and from all walks of life. One common feature in these cases is the manner in which the child speaks to the parent. It is usually in a matter of fact way that the child speaks about the past experience, as though the parent should already know about the events. Phrases are used such as: "Oh look over there, that's where I fell and died."

"I want to be where I was before I came here"
"Not you, the mummy I had before"
"Pretty lady, just like my last mummy".

We have noted that nearly, although not all, of these children speak of a life that appeared to have been cut short. A medium of the past, Ena Twigg, who was highly respected by many of the clergy, among other notables, for the quality of her work, has written in the past that she too had no real belief or interest in the idea of reincarnation until a particular sitter came to see her. An intelligent man, an agnostic, came for a trance sitting as he was grieving after the passing of his young daughter. He did not give the medium any information, not even his name. The medium went into trance to awaken an hour later to find that her dress was soaking with tears and she saw that the sitter was also crying. He said that, through Ena, he had been talking to his dead daughter for nearly one hour in which she gave her name, when, and how she died, amongst other information. The man was confused as he could not understand how this was possible and asked if he could bring a vicar to see Mrs Twigg. Naturally she agreed, although no time was set for this meeting.

Ten days after this sitting in London, a "child", a little girl, appeared at the foot of Ena's bed. Ena noted that it was around midnight. The child asked if Ena could see her, to which she replied that she could, and then the girl asked if she, the medium, would give her "Daddy" a message. It was evident to Ena at this point that she was the daughter of the sitter previously mentioned. The message given by the child to Ena was "Tell my Daddy that tonight I am being born again." She disappeared before any more could be said, but the problem was that Ena did not know how to contact the aforesaid gentleman as he had come to her for a sitting and, as previously stated, she did not even know his name.

Approximately three weeks later when Ena was working in the same place in London, her first sitter proved to be a vicar and yes it turned out to be the friend of the man from four weeks ago. She told the vicar of the child's visit and was astonished by his response. The mother of the "dead" child had given birth to a baby girl, two months prematurely, shortly after midnight on the same evening as the "spirit" girl gave Ena the message for her Daddy. Remember the message "Tell my Daddy that tonight I am being born again."

The vicar was also astonished by the events.

Would you say that this was coincidence?

Chapter 8

PARANORMAL HEALING

Yet another facet of experience that would appear to be true, is that discarnate personalities can assist people on Earth in healing the sick or injured. Many healers claim that 'someone' works 'through' them.

Apart from religious examples there are actually so many instances of this that I will choose only three.

> George Chapman
> Gary Mannion
> Nina Knowland.

George Chapman was a fireman who had little or no medical training. He discovered that he had the ability to heal people, often in the form of psychic surgery. He would go into trance and initially this *persona* told people that he was Dr William Lang from Moorfields Eye Hospital. On subsequent checking it was found that William Lang FRCS really did exist and was a noted ophthalmic specialist in Moorfields Eye Hospital in Middlesex in the latter half of the 19th and early half of the 20th centuries. When Dr Lang worked through Chapman, his appearance would change into that of a slightly taller, older man. Lang would speak and work with patients with his eyes completely shut throughout the whole proceedings. Lang's speciality was in the ophthalmic department, and in fact he had been a Consultant before his demise. When patients arrived with other complaints, rather than eyes, he said that he engaged the help of a team of 'spirit' surgeons, whose speciality was in that particular area and they would work through him.

A journalist, J. Bernard Hutton, had a very bad eye complaint and was in danger of going blind very quickly, when his wife saw an advert for George Chapman's healing clinic. She tried to persuade him to go to the clinic, but he scoffed at the idea. After some persuasion he reluctantly attended the clinic, expressing the opinion that it was all nonsense. This opinion did not change when he saw what appeared to be an old man speaking to him with his eyes tightly shut. After lying down on a table his opinion was nurtured by the fact that this strange man was making passing movements over his eyes, as if he was operating. He was almost at the point of laughing out loud, while stifling his amusement, when things began to change. He began to 'feel' as though someone was working on and inside his eyes.

The outcome was that from that day onward his eyes became slowly better until they levelled out and maintained at a reasonable level of vision for many years to come. He saw some immediate improvement within one hour of the treatment.

So sceptical was he of his improvement that he later asked Chapman for permission to examine his (meticulous) files. Chapman gladly agreed. A book called Healing Hands was produced from this study and really is a 'must read' for anyone who wishes to look deeper into this subject. The book tells of the hundreds of healings that Hutton checked up. All were genuine, as was his own. Chapman healed in this way for around 50 years and only died in 2006.

Healing falls into different categories:

Absent, or distant, healing where directed intention is in some way projected to help a recipient make a recovery.

Hands on healing, the laying on of hands within or without a religious context.

Psychic surgery, with or without the use of implements.

Many absent healing studies have been carried out, in many cases by medical doctors, including Dr Randolph Byrd and Dr Daniel Benor. These were blind studies which mean that the patients did not know if they were in the group that was being sent healing, or in the control group. Benor also reviewed 61 such studies and concluded that healing in a religious context was no more efficacious than outside a religious context. To date there have been more than 150 scientific studies and more than half of them show significant effects.

One study showed that the overall results for 16 double blind trials was-

For prayer, the probability of the results being due to chance was 0.0009.

For distant healing (non-religious directed intention), the probability of the results being due to chance was 0.0003.

These are highly significant results.

Other well-known healers, who obtained apparent surgical results with their healing, are Harry Edwards, Arigo, Edivaldo and John of God. All of these healers maintained that at least one discarnate person was working through them.

The common factors noted for all healers were that;

> The patients feel no fear
> They have little (if any) discomfort
> No actual anaesthetic is used

In over 40 years no infections whatsoever have been reported from patients of any of these people and other genuine psychic surgeons, whether an implement was used or not.

Some people had an appropriate surgical scar in the area of the operation whether or not an instrument was used.

The work of these people, and many others, does not have a sell-by date. Each of these healers has been thoroughly investigated by people who were initially sceptical, but who had to revise their opinion in light of the evidence. There is an enormous amount of data available on this work.

I have been examining two healers, Nina Knowland and Gary Mannion by carrying out controlled research with both of these people from 2007 to 2011, although the preparation for this work began in 2006.

I was made aware of the claims of these healers through a telephone call from Nina, in 2006. I asked her to send me some of her previous patients' details and claims of healing. She willingly did so. At this point I thought that she was either overstating her case or that she may be deluded, although I was convinced by her sincerity. I applied to a psychical research organisation, PRISM, for funding to actively pursue the claims. They agreed to fund travel expenses and so the study began.

Each healer had to employ a strict protocol, designed by me, over this period of time. When travelling to England to pursue this work I was accompanied by Professor Archie Roy. As with case investigations, researchers should always work with at least one other person, even if only to have them as a witness. Part of the protocol requires that, where appropriate, the patient provides a hospital letter, a doctor's letter, a copy of x-rays, or any other relevant medical background.

The above is an over simplification, due to available space in this book - the protocol sheets alone would take up two pages. Every patient's post healing testimony, documentation and video interview, where applicable, is held by myself.

After the first two sessions with Nina, the occupations of the patients thus far ranged from a Bishop's secretary to a bartender. The latter had one of his eyes completely cut through by a broken one pint Guinness glass to such an extent that the retina was detached, the iris was cut through and there was no pressure in the eye. One day after the healing and the day before that patient was due to have the eye removed and replaced with a glass eye, the pressure had returned and the retina had reattached. No operation was then necessary. The patient himself had no belief in anything like this and is still stunned to this day. At this point I had examined the data for 26 patients.

Common factors noted at this time were that;

> 86% of patients felt intense heat from the healer's hands
> 80% had a very quick cessation of pain
> 37% felt a popping, bubbling or fluttering sensation inside them.
> 20% had a feeling of 'someone' working inside their body.

After the first controlled session with the second healer, Gary Mannion, in Glasgow

> 46% reported immediate betterment with their condition
> 13% reported betterment within a few days to a week

The following are further examples of healing carried out by either Gary or Nina.

The first is of a very tall 50 year-old woman who had fallen in her bath two years ago, striking her spine on the side of the bath as she fell. The patient is a highly qualified nurse. She crushed her vertebrae - T10 damaged, actually crushed and inoperable and fractured T12. For two years she had taken maximum dosage of painkillers every 4 hours. The patient felt relief in one session. The following day her husband contacted me to say that she had slept soundly and did not have to take painkillers during the night (which had been unheard of for the past two years). In her interview immediately after the healing she reported that during the healing she felt 'lots of pins and scraping and a scraping noise all the way down to just above the base of my spine. It was uncomfortable but not sore. The pins were like tapping all the way down-from my acupuncture training it felt a bit like that, and then Gary worked up my spine to the base of my skull. When I arrived I had not taken any painkillers and I had numbness in my leg. Right now it is easier already.' 44 days after the healing the report was 'The healing has been nothing short of amazing, no pain whatsoever where the injuries were.' Five months later she was still feeling fine. This appears to have been maintained to date.

Another patient was a lady journalist who had been unable to lead a normal life for 30 years due to a vertigo type condition because of crystals in her ears. This meant that when she stood or walked she was unbalanced and nauseous. There was no form of medical treatment offered during this time. After one healing with Gary she told me "At the age of 63 I have my life back, my husband has his wife back, and it is wonderful." That was four years ago and her condition has never come back.

In December 2008, a 19 month child was brought to Nina. She had very bad eczema, mainly on her back and behind her knees, since birth. The medical establishment could only offer a selection of steroid creams for the condition. Each time a new cream was tried the mother cultivated the habit of taking a picture of the child's back before applying the new cream and she would then take pictures of it at regular intervals to see if there was any discernible improvement. As the girl was now 19 months old the mother thought that this was ridiculous as she did not want to keep applying steroid cream to her child. In desperation she took the child to Nina. It is important to note that the child was asleep when taken in for healing, she slept all through the healing and was still asleep when the mother took her home, therefore she did not know that anything different had taken place. Between 24 and 36 hours later the eczema had completely disappeared and has never come back. I telephoned the mother in 2011 to check that this was still the case and received an affirmative answer.

The research covered, in total, 130 varying conditions:

Skeletal 44
Organic 23
Emotionally based 4
Mixed cases 59

Of these, 101 conditions showed improvement in one visit

78 patients experienced heat from the healer's hands
46 felt some kind of internal movement during the healing
46 experienced a quick cessation of pain.
2 felt as though they had an anaesthetic.

These numbers reflect the fact that patients had more than one experience during healing.

Gary appears to achieve outstanding results with skeletal and muscular conditions although others are also worthy. Nina achieves good results with gallstones, haemorrhoids and female conditions, although the healing of Shaun's eye was outstanding. Emotionally based conditions do not seem to have the same level of success.

For those who wish to say that the patients would have improved anyway - isn't it strange how the betterment occurred immediately or soon after the healings? One case on its own does not necessarily indicate that anything unusual is happening, but when the cases are bound together it must tell us that 'something is going on'."

Some more examples:

Man aged 21 d.o.b. 03/06/78

Condition Compression fractures (schmals) T6/T7/T8; scoliosis 15 degrees convex to RHSConsultant – South Africa

Occupation – electrician

Patient felt heat, tingling, internal movement, external movement, sewing sensation, relaxed, pulling sensation.
Healer felt heat, tingling, internal movement, external

movement, cutting sensation, sewing sensation, relaxation, vibrating hands, pulling sensation, grinding sounds and an emotional release in the patient.

Testimony "Before consulting Gary Mannion I was experiencing pain due to previous back injuries (compression fractures of T6, 7, 8: impacted coccyx; scoliosis and muscle tension as a result of misaligned vertebra). At the time I had been suffering the injury for 10 years.

I lay down in a prone position and as Gary began working on me I felt what can be described as electrostatic shocks in my back, and the sensation that the vertebra were being moved in my back. While Gary was working on me he said that my hips were misaligned and this was causing the majority of my discomfort and this would be rectified first. When I got up from the plinth I asked Gary if he was holding anything in his hands, he replied "no" and rolled up his sleeves to prove this. As I stood up I immediately noticed that the elasticity had returned to my hips and my pain could no longer be felt. There was an approximate 80% reduction in my pain and improvement in my postural alignment that cannot be easily described, except that I was walking with more ease. Upon my return home I took off my T shirt and four of my relatives remarked that there was an imprint of my spine on the skin of my back. This was not painful at all and disappeared in 24 hours.

After 2 more appointments there was an overall and lasting improvement (90%) in my condition and the reduction of pain in general. Today is approximately one year after the first consultation with Gary - and I am still feeling lasting benefit of the healing consultation."

Patient, man aged 53. Surrey. Healing date 13/09/08

Conditions being treated
1 Kidney tired
2 Post-op internal scar tissue
3 Post-op pain removal from fluid build up after vein removal
Consultant condition 1 James P*** Guy's Hospital
Consultant condition 2 and condition 3 Prof Jan G *** St George's

Medication
1. Aspirin and betablockers 2. Predrisolene azathioprine.
3. Nothing
2. Occupation – Company Director.

Condition 1 During the healing felt heat, internal movement, stretching, pulling sensation, trembling, Improvement in one visit.

Condition 2 felt heat, tingling, internal movement other hands inside his body, fluttering, gentle smoothing, Improvement in one visit.

Condition 3 felt heat, relaxation, pulling sensation, fluttering, gentle smoothing. Improvement in one visit.

Healer felt heat with each condition and internal movement with condition 1. Healer felt no change in consciousness.

Different male patient.

Testimony
Potted medical history
August 1976 chronic renal failure following a car accident 6 months earlier
Feb 1979 double nephrectomy
April 1979 live kidney transplant from mother
June 1999 Heart attack
Sept 1999 Stent operation
Dec 2007 June 2008 angina problems
June 2008 Quadruple by-pass
Reasons for visiting Gary:-
Post-op pain in left leg and severe swelling, where the veins were removed for heart surgery. Large swelling/lump at the base of the rib cage. In addition the transplanted kidney is beginning to fail.

Day after the healing the patient wrote: 'Feeling very good if a little tired (didn't get up till 11.30 this morning, which is very unusual for me! The 'lump' at the end of my chest scar has gone. No pain restriction when stretching! Fantastic!! I will send you a medical history by post this week.'

Follow up testimony
Since your treatment I have no lump at the base of my chest, which disappeared immediately after the session, my leg swelling has reduced

to nothing and I'm peeing like a racehorse! I am due to see the kidney specialists and heart surgeons in October which will be interesting. Once again thanks for your amazing help. I keep saying, I don't know how you do it, but it works for me.

Hand written testimony, Fred S. Age 43. I have copies of the x -rays

On 17th Sept 2006 a concrete and cast iron manhole cover came down on his arms. He went to hospital and they x-rayed the ulna and the radius.

"I had two operations on my arm, on the 18th and the 21st Sept. and they set it in plaster. I had two casts but the bone didn't fuse together and over a period of time it calcified. The next x-ray on the 5th Oct showed that the bone was not mending".

Two x-rays on the 2nd Nov show more calcium build up around the bone.

X –rays on 30th Nov show more calcium build up and the bones seem to be pulling apart.

Following another x-ray on 11th January 2007 they decided that they were going to break the arm again, take a piece from my pelvis, pin it and do a bone graft. (called pin and plate)

A few days later Nina gave him healing. "Later in January I went back into hospital for another x-ray, they decided they did not need to break my arm, they were satisfied that it was OK. The final x-ray showed the calcium had gone away and the bone was perfect. I believe through Nina's healing, my arm is now mended and I am able to return to work."

During the healing the patient just felt an ache in his arm.

The healer felt no change in consciousness, just heat going from her hands to the patient.

Healing date 8th Nov 2009
36 year old woman

Condition, Persistent Lichen Sclerosis Like auto-immune disease affecting the vulva area, like eczema, causes a lace appearance scarring to the skin. Splits and bleeds. Painful on urinating, itching. Worse when it is hormone related during a period.

Consultant Miss McN***, Oncology dept. Musgrove.
Medication painkillers, amitriptyline, steroid cream
Medical letters – yes
Improvement in one visit?
Yes, irritation and itching stopped. Stopped splitting and bleeding.
Patient felt heat, internal movement, urinating feeling fluttering – like a baby turning

Patient's Written Testimony date 19th November 2009
'I laid on mum's bed and Nina placed her hands on my lower abdomen over my ovaries, her hands became very hot I started to feel sensations below which felt as if I was urinating. The next day my symptoms were very painful, similar to how I felt after visiting the hospital when I first had the condition, the hospital had removed a layer of skin from the vulva which left a burning sensation.
The following day I looked at the area and it was white…there was no lacy scarring, no itching. I thought that this may change when I had my next period but it didn't which is very unusual. It has been 11 days and I have had no symptoms of the Lichen sclerosis.'
I spoke to patient early 2010. She has had no recurrence of condition. She is due to see consultant soon and will keep me updated.

Follow up written testimony 19/5/10
"It has been about 6 months since having healing with Nina. My symptoms of the lichen sclerosis have not come back. I had an appointment with the oncologist in March this year. They photograph the area and compare from the photographs of previous visits. She asked what creams I was using. I told her I had stopped the steroid and Amitriptyline. She was not pleased about that. She was however amazed that there is an improvement in the condition, it appears to have become dormant. I told her about the healing and she said not to attribute the significant change as to anything else apart from good fortune - the condition will always be present. Normally when you get this condition there is no cure for it .They can only treat the symptoms for comfort. Being without this condition has been like I have never had it apart from scarring where the biopsy had been taken. Miss McN***, the Consultant Oncologist, is one of the top consultants for this condition in the country."
Gary and Nina take no credit for the healings, but simply feel that discarnate people are working through them. Having met and worked

with these two healers I can only confirm their sincerity as they conduct their work. Subsequent to the study I have witnessed many more amazing healings.

You know the old saying 'Don't knock it until you've tried it'

Chapter 9

SUMMING UP

As stated earlier, psychical research is a careful, rational, systematic study of the alleged paranormal or anomalous phenomena and began in earnest in London with the creation, in January 1882, of the Society for Psychical Research. (S.P.R) Although individual scientists of the calibre of Sir William Crookes and Sir William Barrett had conducted studies of mediums, there was obviously a need for a coordinated approach to the subject. The setting up of a society with lectures, a journal and a proceedings and a carefully chosen council seemed the appropriate thing to do.

Throughout its existence to the present date, the S.P.R. has enjoyed the allegiance and expertise of some of the most gifted scientists, psychologists, physicians, philosophers and statesmen. As Brian Inglis, in his foreword to Dr Alan Gauld's book puts it: There can be few organisations that have attracted so distinguished a membership. Among physicists have been Sir William Crookes, Sir John Joseph Thomson, Sir Oliver Lodge, Sir William Barrett and two Lord Rayleighs - the third and fourth Barons. Among the philosophers: Sidgwick himself, Henri Bergson, Ferdinand Schiller, L.P.Jacks, Hans Driesch and C. D. Broad; among the psychologists: William James, Sigmund Freud, Walter Franklin Prince, Carl Jung and Gardner Murphy. And along with these have been many eminent figures in various fields: Charles Richet, a Nobel prize-winner in physiology; the Earl of Balfour, Prime Minister from 1902-6, and his brother Gerald, Chief Secretary for Ireland in 1895-6; Andrew Lang, polymath; Gilbert Murray, Regis Professor of Greek at Oxford and drafter of the first Covenant of the League of Nations; his successor at Oxford, E.R.Dodds; Mrs Henry Sidgwick, Principal of Newnham College, Cambridge; Marie Curie; the Hon Mrs Alfred Lyttelton, Delegate to the League of Nations Assembly; Camille Flammarion, the astronomer, and F. J. M. Stratton, president of the Royal Astronomical Society; and Sir Alister Hardy, Professor of Zoology at Oxford.

Such a list, as Arthur Koestler pointed out, 'ought to be sufficient to demonstrate that ESP research ' is not a playground for superstitious cranks'. On the contrary, the standards of research have in general been rigorous - far more rigorous, as psychologists have on occasion had to admit, than those of psychology.'

To put it another way: in the first century of the S.P.R.'s existence, among the 51 Presidents of the Society there were 19 Professors, 10 Fellows of the Royal Society, 5 Fellows of the British Academy, 4 holders of the Order of Merit and one Nobel prize-winner.

One can only think...Phew! after that list, and be encouraged by the thought that all of these great thinkers were interested in the same questions as we are.

We have looked at the questions...   What are we as human beings? Is there any evidence that may show that our personality may survive physical death? I wonder if I have given you food for thought, or an interest in pursuing the topics further. It would also be interesting to know if your opinions have altered since reading these accounts.

This book only gives a taste of peoples' experiences with paranormal phenomena and perhaps, in some cases, with the departed and is certainly not at all comprehensive. I would recommend that, if you are really interested, that you continue to read reliable books on these particular individual topics along with many others such as Near Death Experience, Precognition, and Telepathy etc. While doing so also remember the pedigree of the people from the past who have examined these things from an experiential or pragmatic standpoint. So if you choose to think that I am slightly mad, then I am in good company.

I hope that I have opened your mind with the contents of this book and can only reiterate that everything contained in it is written with 100% honesty. Fortunately, I have no mediumistic abilities whatsoever and no inclination to pursue them. I also had no great need to examine these things initially as I had no recent bereavement or any other 'need', only an intellectual interest followed by the pursuit of evidence either for or against any particular paranormal topic. There is an enormous wealth of evidence out there to be harvested. Do not be put off by the well-known television sceptics, paid to do so, who are brought out to play the part of a sceptic as programme directors seem to feel the need for this. They usually hold up a weak case and, quite correctly, discredit it, but that is not the true picture for other cases. Every claim of paranormality must be judged on its own merits by examining the evidence, as in a court of law, i.e. beyond reasonable doubt.

It would certainly appear to me that the departed can, on occasions, communicate in various ways, with those left behind. With modern technology, people are claiming to have communications through computers, telephones, answer machines, recorders etc. The evidence should tell us, through time, if this is correct or not.

The only 'proof' of these matters is in experience; nothing will be achieved in a laboratory with students as subjects. Life is all about emotion; survival seems to be the same in that emotion and intention seem to be the underlying factors, or principles for some kind of communication.

Chapter 10

IMPLICATIONS

Wo hat can we make of the phenomena reported in spontaneous cases?

If we are to accept as true and accurate, sensibly and carefully investigated accounts of cases recorded, not only in this book but in hundreds of others, then surely the sensible person would have to study the implications of such an acceptance.

What are the implications?

Beginning with the movement of objects as described in the poltergeist cases, and rather violent movement at that in many of the cases including the Fife, Enfield and Cardiff cases, we would have to consider the implication that some unseen force or energy must be causing the movements, as nothing can be moved without an energy source. In scientific terms energy is defined as the capacity to do work, therefore "something" gives these items the capacity (ability) to move, even the very loud sound of the thwacking coming from the headboard in the Fife case has to have a cause and a methodology for producing the sound.

The source of energy in each of the above cases may be quite different, but leaving that aside, an energy source must be present if movement occurs. This source may not be explainable or quantifiable by our accepted scientific standards at the present time, but does this mean that we should ignore it? Newton knew and theorised that two masses would always be attracted to each other, but initially he had no idea why. The actual theory was produced later.

Nothing "new" in scientific discoveries was ever achieved without a substantial section of the establishment thinking that the author/inventor was deluded and misguided. Many people seem desperate to protect the status quo of their knowledge, or world model, displaying a tremendous inertia which could possibly be described as a protective device; one might call it (as previously said) with the "Do not confuse me with facts, my mind is made up" syndrome.

If we accept the fact that spontaneous events also throw up genuine phenomena, which cannot be explained in a normal manner, and that some of the phenomena are from a source other than a living human being, then surely the logical step would be to ask the question, how can we progress our understanding if these matters?

Does this further the idea that there is a part of a human being which in a real sense survives death and that human personality lives on in an active and vibrant way in some non - physical sense, maintaining all of his/her individual memories, intellect and personality? A hundred years ago most people would not have been able to accept this in any rational way, but with all the twentieth and twenty-first century's discoveries in quantum theory, plasma physics, wave and other particle physics, which have in a real sense dematerialised the physical world, the concept of a non-physical existence does not sound quite so crazy as perhaps it may have in the past.

BIBLIOGRAPHY

The books, or papers, listed in the bibliography contain books that are referred to in this book or are recommendations for further reading.

JSPR/PSPR *Journal/Proceedings of the Society for Psychical Research*

JASPR/PASPR *Journal/Proceedings of the American Society for Psychical Research*

Braude, S.E. 2003 *Immortal Remains, The Evidence for Life After Death.* Rowman and Littlefield.

Cooper, Cal. 2012 *Telephone Calls From the Dead.* Tricorn Books.

Findlay, Arthur. 1953 *On the Edge of the Etheric, The Rock of Truth, Looking Back, The Way of Life.* WBC Print Ltd.

Fontana, D. 1991 *A Responsive Poltergeist: a case from South Wales.* JSPR 57, 385-403.

Fontana, D. 2009 *Life Beyond Death, What Should We Expect?.* Watkins Publishing.

Fuller, J. G. 1981 *The Airmen Who would not Die,* Corgi, London.

Fuller, J.G. 1974 *Arigo: Surgeon of the Rusty Knife,* Hart-Davis, MacGibbon.

Gauld, A. 1966-72 *A Series of 'Drop-in' Communicators*, PSPR 55, 273-340.

Gauld, A. 1968 *The Founders of Psychical Research*. London: Routledge and Kegan Paul .

Gauld, A. and Cornell, A.D.1979 *Poltergeists*. London and Boston: Routledge & Kegan Paul

Gauld, A. 1982. *Mediumship and Survival*. Heinemann, London.

Gurney, E., Myers, F.W.H., and Podmore, F. 1886. *Phantasms of the Living*, vols. 1 and 2. The Society for Psychical Research and Trubner and Company.

Hamilton, T. 2012 *Tell My Mother I'm not Dead*. Imprint Academic.

Haraldsson, E. 2000 Birthmarks and Claims of Previous-Life Memories. 1. The Case of Purnima Ekanayake. JSPR, 64.1, 16-25.

Haraldsson, E. and Stevenson, I. 1975, A Communicator of the 'Drop-in' type in Iceland: The Case of Runolfur Runolfsson. JASPR 69, 35-59.

Haraldsson, E. and Stevenson, I. 1975, A Communicator of the 'Drop-in' type in Iceland: The Case of Gudni Magnusson. JASPR 69, 245-261.

Hutton J B 1978 *Healing Hands*. W.H. Allen.

Hyslop, J.H. 1909. A Case of Veridical Hallucinations, PASPR 3, 1-469.

Inglis, Brian. 1977 *Natural and Supernatural*, Hodder and Stoughton.

Inglis, Brian. 1984 *Science and Parascience,* Hodder and Stoughton.

Inglis, Brian 1985 *The Paranormal*, Granada, London.

Ireland, M 2010 *Soul Shift*. Frog Books.

Lodge, O. 1909 *Survival of Man*, Methuen, London.

Lodge, O. 1911 Evidence of Classical Scholarship and of Cross- Correspondence in some New Automatic Writing. PSPR 25. 129-142.

Mackenzie, A. 1971 *Apparitions and Ghosts*. Arthur Barker, London.

Piper, A.L. 1929 *The Life and Work of Mrs Piper.* London: Kegan Paul.

Playfair, G.L. 2011 *This House is Haunted*, White Crow Books, Guildford.

Playfair, G.L. and Grosse, M. 1988 Enfield Revisited, JSPR 55, 50-78.

Playfair, G.L. 2012 *Twin Telepathy*. White Crow Books, Guildford.

Playfair, G. L. 2011 *Chico Xavier, Medium of the Century.* Roundtable publishing.

Richet, C. 1923. *Thirty Years of Psychical Research: Being a Treatise on Metapsychics* (S. de Brath, Trans.) New York: MacMillan.

Robertson T.J. and Roy A.E. 2001, A preliminary Study of the Acceptance by Non-Recipients of Mediums' Statements to Recipients. JSPR 65.2 91-106

Roy A.E. and T.J Robertson 2001, A Double Blind Procedure for assessing The Relevance of a Medium's Statements to a Recipient. JSPR 65.3 161-74

Robertson T.J. and Roy A.E. 2004, Results of the Application of the Robertson-Roy Protocol to a series of Experiments with Mediums and Participants. JSPR 68.1 18-34

Rogo, D. Scott, 1979 *The Poltergeist Experience.* Penguin books, Baltimore (USA).

Rogo, D. Scott, 1988 The Infinite Boundary. The Aquarian Press: Wellingborough.

Roy, A.E. 1996 *The Archives of the Mind.* Psychic Press, Stansted.

Roy, A.E. 2008. *The Eager Dead,* Book Guild.

Stemman, R.2012 *The Big Book Of Reincarnation,* Hierophant Publishing.

Stevenson, I. Are Poltergeists Living or are They Dead? 1972 JASPR 66, 233 - 252.

Stevenson, I. 1974 *Twenty Cases Suggestive of Reincarnation,* University of Virginia Press, Charlottesville.

Stevenson, I. 1975 *Cases of the Reincarnation Type. Vol. 1. Ten Cases in India.* Charlottesville: University Press of Virginia.

Stevenson, I. 1977 *Cases of the Reincarnation Type. Vol. 2. Ten Cases in Sri Lanka.* Charlottesville: University Press of Virginia.

Stevenson, I. 1980 *Cases of the Reincarnation Type. Vol. 3. Twelve Cases in Lebanon and Turkey.* Charlottesville: University Press of Virginia.

Stevenson, I. 1987 *Children Who Remember Previous Lives.* Charlottesville: University Press of Virginia.

Wilson, C. 1982 *Poltergeist,* New English Library, London.

ABOUT TRICIA

A former teacher of mathematics and physics Tricia is a long term council member, past Vice President and Immediate Past President of the Scottish Society for Psychical Research.

She is a tutor for the Department of Adult and Continuing Education (DACE) at the University of Glasgow. In conjunction with Professor Archie Roy she provided a session programme of 20, 2 hour, lectures per session for DACE in a series entitled "An In Depth Study of Psychical Research." This course has now been running for six years. The paranormal- what is the evidence?'

In addition to 29 years of experience in investigating spontaneous cases Tricia has appeared on various radio and TV programmes and has been invited, over many of years, to speak to varied organisations throughout the U K.

She has written the forward to Dr Mark Ireland's highly successful book *Soul Shift*, and some of her comments are on the back cover of Trevor Hamilton's book *Tell my Mother I am not Dead*.

She has a wealth of experience in investigating spontaneous cases and has done so for around 30 years. Tricia is known as an interesting speaker on many topics concerning psychical research, which is reflected by the invitations that she receives from varied avenues.

Lectures in recent years include:
Various plus The 'Gwen Tate' Lecture for the SPR in London, in October 2005

The Glastonbury Symposium 2006
SPR Study Day presentation 2006
The Ghost Club, London, 2006
The Theosophical Society of Edinburgh, 2005
The Churches Fellowship for Psychic and Spiritual Studies- on various occasions
The Edinburgh College of Parapsychology- various occasions
The Ayrshire Association for Spiritual Knowledge-yearly since 1989- June 2008
Muncaster Castle Conference 2004
The Lynwood Fellowship-various occasions
Stirling association of spiritual knowledge-various occasions last one Sept 2008
The West of Scotland Dowsers- various occasions
Presidential Address for the SSPR 2005
Unitarian Church , Glasgow 2005, 2006, 2007, 2008
A lecture to Mensa at Malvern 2006
Lecture to A.S.K , Dreghorn, June 2009
A Gwen Tate Lecture for the SPR London October 2009
Norwegian Parapsychological Soc 2010
Lecture to Quakers in Oxford Oct 2010
Invited speaker to the International conference of the London based SPR 2011
Invited speaker at SPR Study Day 2012
Speaker for West of Scotland Dowsers 2013
Speaker for Arthur Conan Doyle Centre 2013
Invited speaker for SPR Study Day 2013

Presentation of many papers to the SPR International Conference, last one - September 2009

Research

Along with many television appearances, normally in documentaries, since 1990 she has also prepared and presented many papers to the SPR International Conferences, over the past 20 years.

She is the co-author, with Professor Archie Roy, of three published papers on the study of information provided by mediums. These papers follow a five-year study of controlled experiments in conditions up to triple blind. The results of these studies are published in the JSPR April 2001, January 2004 and July 2004.

Tricia was a founding member, and Hon Sec of PRISM, Psychical Research Involving Selected Mediums, 1994- 2008.

She has completed a four/five year, in depth, study of exceptional paranormal healing, started 2006 and producing some spectacular results. Some of these results would indicate a form of psychic surgery. The final report may be downloaded from this site.

She has completed a report on a 6 year old boy in Scotland, who remembers a previous life.

Apart from three published peer reviewed papers in the JSPR, she has articles published in the journals of the Swedish and Norwegian Societies for Psychical Research.

Tricia is passionate about the evidence gathered in various aspects of Psychical Research, and does not suffer fools gladly who will not address specific evidence in any particular avenue.

While accepting that some people may be deluded in some aspects of experience, it is certain that there are genuine cases in nearly every aspect of paranormal claims.

Paperbacks also available from
White Crow Books

Elsa Barker—*Letters from
a Living Dead Man*
ISBN 978-1-907355-83-7

Elsa Barker—*War Letters from
the Living Dead Man*
ISBN 978-1-907355-85-1

Elsa Barker—*Last Letters from
the Living Dead Man*
ISBN 978-1-907355-87-5

Richard Maurice Bucke—
Cosmic Consciousness
ISBN 978-1-907355-10-3

Arthur Conan Doyle—
The Edge of the Unknown
ISBN 978-1-907355-14-1

Arthur Conan Doyle—
The New Revelation
ISBN 978-1-907355-12-7

Arthur Conan Doyle—
The Vital Message
ISBN 978-1-907355-13-4

Arthur Conan Doyle with
Simon Parke—*Conversations
with Arthur Conan Doyle*
ISBN 978-1-907355-80-6

Meister Eckhart with Simon Parke—
Conversations with Meister Eckhart
ISBN 978-1-907355-18-9

D. D. Home—*Incidents in my Life Part 1*
ISBN 978-1-907355-15-8

Mme. Dunglas Home; edited,
with an Introduction, by Sir
Arthur Conan Doyle—*D. D.
Home: His Life and Mission*
ISBN 978-1-907355-16-5

Edward C. Randall—
Frontiers of the Afterlife
ISBN 978-1-907355-30-1

Rebecca Ruter Springer—
Intra Muros: My Dream of Heaven
ISBN 978-1-907355-11-0

Leo Tolstoy, edited by Simon
Parke—*Forbidden Words*
ISBN 978-1-907355-00-4

Leo Tolstoy—*A Confession*
ISBN 978-1-907355-24-0

Leo Tolstoy—*The Gospel in Brief*
ISBN 978-1-907355-22-6

Leo Tolstoy—*The Kingdom
of God is Within You*
ISBN 978-1-907355-27-1

Leo Tolstoy—*My Religion:
What I Believe*
ISBN 978-1-907355-23-3

Leo Tolstoy—*On Life*
ISBN 978-1-907355-91-2

Leo Tolstoy—*Twenty-three Tales*
ISBN 978-1-907355-29-5

Leo Tolstoy—*What is Religion
and other writings*
ISBN 978-1-907355-28-8

Leo Tolstoy—*Work While
Ye Have the Light*
ISBN 978-1-907355-26-4

Leo Tolstoy—*The Death of Ivan Ilyich*
ISBN 978-1-907661-10-5

Leo Tolstoy—*Resurrection*
ISBN 978-1-907661-09-9

Leo Tolstoy with Simon Parke—
Conversations with Tolstoy
ISBN 978-1-907355-25-7

Howard Williams with an Introduction
by Leo Tolstoy—*The Ethics of Diet:
An Anthology of Vegetarian Thought*
ISBN 978-1-907355-21-9

Vincent Van Gogh with Simon
Parke—*Conversations with Van Gogh*
ISBN 978-1-907355-95-0

Wolfgang Amadeus Mozart with Simon
Parke—*Conversations with Mozart*
ISBN 978-1-907661-38-9

Jesus of Nazareth with Simon Parke—
Conversations with Jesus of Nazareth
ISBN 978-1-907661-41-9

Thomas à Kempis with Simon
Parke—*The Imitation of Christ*
ISBN 978-1-907661-58-7

Julian of Norwich with Simon
Parke—*Revelations of Divine Love*
ISBN 978-1-907661-88-4

Allan Kardec—*The Spirits Book*
ISBN 978-1-907355-98-1

Allan Kardec—*The Book on Mediums*
ISBN 978-1-907661-75-4

Emanuel Swedenborg—*Heaven and Hell*
ISBN 978-1-907661-55-6

P.D. Ouspensky—*Tertium Organum:
The Third Canon of Thought*
ISBN 978-1-907661-47-1

Dwight Goddard—*A Buddhist Bible*
ISBN 978-1-907661-44-0

Michael Tymn—*The Afterlife Revealed*
ISBN 978-1-970661-90-7

Michael Tymn—*Transcending the
Titanic: Beyond Death's Door*
ISBN 978-1-908733-02-3

Guy L. Playfair—*If This Be Magic*
ISBN 978-1-907661-84-6

Guy L. Playfair—*The Flying Cow*
ISBN 978-1-907661-94-5

Guy L. Playfair —*This House is Haunted*
ISBN 978-1-907661-78-5

Carl Wickland, M.D.—
Thirty Years Among the Dead
ISBN 978-1-907661-72-3

John E. Mack—*Passport to the Cosmos*
ISBN 978-1-907661-81-5

Peter & Elizabeth Fenwick—
The Truth in the Light
ISBN 978-1-908733-08-5

Erlendur Haraldsson—
Modern Miracles
ISBN 978-1-908733-25-2

Erlendur Haraldsson—
At the Hour of Death
ISBN 978-1-908733-27-6

Erlendur Haraldsson—
The Departed Among the Living
ISBN 978-1-908733-29-0

Brian Inglis—*Science and Parascience*
ISBN 978-1-908733-18-4

Brian Inglis—*Natural and Supernatural:
A History of the Paranormal*
ISBN 978-1-908733-20-7

Ernest Holmes—*The Science of Mind*
ISBN 978-1-908733-10-8

Victor Zammit—*Afterlife: A
Lawyer Presents the Evidence.*
ISBN 978-1-908733-22-1

Casper S. Yost—*Patience
Worth: A Psychic Mystery*
ISBN 978-1-908733-06-1

William Usborne Moore—
Glimpses of the Next State
ISBN 978-1-907661-01-3

William Usborne Moore—
The Voices
ISBN 978-1-908733-04-7

John W. White—
The Highest State of Consciousness
ISBN 978-1-908733-31-3

Stafford Betty—
The Imprisoned Splendor
ISBN 978-1-907661-98-3

Paul Pearsall, Ph.D. —
Super Joy
ISBN 978-1-908733-16-0

**All titles available as eBooks, and selected titles available in Hardback and
Audiobook formats from www.whitecrowbooks.com**

CPSIA information can be obtained at www.ICGtesting.com
Printed in the USA
BVOW081130140713

325890BV00001B/142/P